SALTWATER SOULS

personal stories

FROM YOUGHAL'S COMMUNITY OF SEA SWIMMERS

Cover illustration courtesy of Andrea Cashell

Supported by

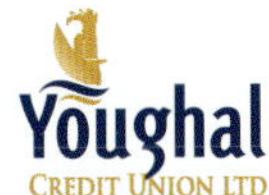

DEDICATION

To the millions of saltwater souls
who have walked and swam on these shores
from the days of the yew wood forest to the present time.
The love of the sea and the connections formed
continue to be nourished to this day.

FOREWORD

Some days calm, some days troubled, the sea never fails to fascinate. Since June 2020, the sea has particularly enchanted our community of sea swimmers. Every day, if it is safe to do so, a pod of swimmers can be seen swimming in the Front Strand here in Youghal, Co. Cork from as early as 6.30am to late evening. But what compels us to wax lyrical about swimming in the sea?

I believe that it is all about making connections. Connecting with nature, connecting with people and connecting with ourselves. It is this innate need to connect that sparked the flame to fan this book. To attempt to capture in printed form what sea swimming means to our community as they brave the elements to swim in our sea. All our swimmers were invited to share their own personal stories on why they sea swim. Submissions were welcomed in a variety of formats and included poems, stories, photographs and artwork.

I always valued the art of storytelling and how it offers us a glimpse into people's lives. It is the sharing of stories that empowers us to make connections. Surely, isn't this what a community strives for? A community that nourishes positive social connections is what our sea swimming group promotes. Hearing the shrieks of laughter from our swimmers as we wade into the cold water in winter is uplifting and invigorating as we find our sense of comfort in the uncomfortable. Feeling the warmth of the sun on our skin in summer creates a calmness that offers us a sense of balance. To float together, to laugh together and swim together is restorative. Sharing a chat, cuppa and treat after our swim is a connection that we value as food for the soul.

Connecting with the sea has sharpened our senses as it displays a palette of colours that often light up the sky. A sense of lightness is felt as we slip and slide with the waves, tasting the briny flavour of sea water. The gentle brush of a sea breeze alerts us to an external force of nature that allows us time to nourish our connection with ourselves. Our swimmers are immensely proud of this book. We love that it offers the reader slices of our lives as we share images of laughter, sadness, comfort, magic and most of all connections with the sea's constant presence.

Linda Donoghue

CREATOR GOD

Thank you for warm sunny days when the sun shines through the clear sea, making diamond patterns on the sand beneath and I stand and marvel at it. When I laze on my back in the sea, I see the body of the sea birds, their open wings, so amazingly made, idling on the thermals. I watch them and I know you made them. Thank you.

I watch fluffy white clouds disappear as the sun's rays dry them up and as I flip over to swim I feel the heat from the sun warming all my body and I say thank you.

Stretching out my body to swim I thank you that I have the health, strength, energy and time to swim.

Thank you too for the days I watch rain drops at eye level splashing into the sea and I watch the tiny, ever circling ripples and other drops join them and splash onto me, it's like a different world in the ever-changing sea.

Thank you for days when the seas pound in crashing waves onto the beach, waves to jump over, or dive under, or get bashed around by and I feel the absolute power of the sea as it swirls all around me, invigorating and energising and my shrieks of laughter are swept away with everyone else's. We rub ourselves with the swathes of seaweed which are supposed to be good for our skin, but no matter, it's great anyway and we laugh together.

Thank you for the days when I feel I could swim forever, full of energy and also for the days when I am so tired and exhausted, yet after my immersion in the sea, I feel less tired and weary and ready to thankfully face the day.

Thank you for the people who invented neoprene hats, gloves and shoes, so I can get into the cold sea and still enjoy it all. Thank you for cosy clothes and dry robes to put on after my swim, for friendly chat and newsy stories, for cups of hot water/tea/coffee, to warm hands and to drink, for cakes and nibbles to eat, for comforting hugs, a caring word, shared enjoyments and experiences and lots and lots of laughter and banter.

Thank you God for all these and for the wonderful tribe of sea swimmers.

Rosemary Grant

TRANQUILITY

The sun sets
On another day
Into the sea
To wash it away.

Cold calm surrounds us
Stony sand underneath
No words can describe
The feeling of peace.

Racing thoughts halt
Fists are unclenched
Muscles relax
The body is drenched.

Weightless in water
Worries disappear
Floating through feelings
Tranquility is here.

Aisling Curran

THE SEA

The sea has allowed me an escape.
To strip off my worries before I get in.
Because my body needs my mind to brave the chill.
The cool water rises slowly up, my toes, my ankles, waist in now, here comes the shrill.
Now, I have become with this ocean, this silver, this blue, this magic potion.

Because it allows me to, it holds me up, swirls me around,
splashes me in the face, makes me smile.
I duck under like a seal, see the sand and stones on the bottom.
Swoosh freely with the tide, float on my back, watch my toes twinkle in the sun,
here is a big wave, wait, ready, jump under!

I look around in swells and see familiar faces.
Hear laughter, feel tears, they all melt together with our breathing into the sea.
For we are beautiful mammals with the knowledge that we are blessed with this grace.

At the rocks and the crocs now, my toes are numb.
I try to get my knickers on without flashing my bum.
No matter, because my heart is much lighter, my soul is warmed up
in dry robes, like penguins we waddle away.
The same magic inside us will bring us all back, to begin a new day.

Vicki Magee

FLOATING BUT GROUNDED;

Space to heal and grow found between the waves.

Post lockdown, walks past layered and wrapped up dippers. Teeth chattering teacups, hot water bottle padding, all worn with glowing faces and laughter rippling around a well-dressed table. Smiling invites to dip or have tea... politely declined... for now. Sometimes, when I'm early, I can hear the screeches and shrieks from prom's end and it causes laughter to bubble up and out spontaneously.

April turned and the first public gathering in Youghal was Darkness into Light for Pieta House. As someone who has been ill with depression, this cause is so deserving of support. Like many, I've also lost friends who have died by suicide and my own experience of the illness has meant a huge life change to maintain my mental health and wellbeing. It seemed that after completing the walk with family, taking my first dip would be an occasion to remember all who still suffer stigma because of the illness and remember with love all those who support me and accept me as I am. The sunrise was glorious, the sea calm and the tide was out. I did swim growing up, so the water wasn't the issue but anxiety was building from when we left Aura at the start of the walk, not around the swim but around walking down a public beach into the sea despite wobbly bits and a crowd observing, I needn't have worried, the first slap of a cold wave and it vanished and I laughed at the idea of me now being one of the 'screamers'. The sea welcomed me gently that morning, as did all the lovely people having the cup afterwards.

Since then, water circle conversations, swim costume fails, gingernut and cheese, Christina Berry bakes and buying extra swimsuits have become part of my day. Sunrise swims, sunset and moonrise swims, double and treble dip days and my introduction to the Diving Rocks, an education in sea swimming. Socially, breakfast on the beach, at the bench, in gardens, mobiles and houses with gracious and welcoming hosts, all made the summer such a special one. A memorable afternoon tea on a long balmy Saturday afternoon was as easy as the company, which is always inclusive and respectful of everyone's space and story.

Water safety in the sea is promoted and education promoting breathwork and stroke was soaked up and practised. Currents, rip tides, offshore winds and high tides, a new vocabulary. Hats and goggles snatching waves, coupled with involuntary sinus washouts, feet snatching tide turning waves causing me to explore the shoreline close up provided a hands-on learning experience. Note to self, you cannot stand up if you are laughing too much. Respect for the sea, especially the sneaky small strong waves, learnings came as quickly as the filling tide. Practising side stroke breathing, swimming to the first, then second groyne, then to the first set of boardwalk steps, Rosemary's gliding backstroke leading the way. Bobbing coloured hats ahead of and beside me, someone is heading for Capel Island, again, not me, for a change. Amid all this activity, was a huge discovery.

Floating! Not just for breath calming, but something deeper. I learned to dive under waves or pause as they pass over. Then there is a space before the next wave rolls in where breath can be taken. But what I have found in that space is a stillness which is amplified when I float. Held by the sea reflecting the sky, calming breath, heart and mind finding stillness. A grounding experience (without the ground) which brings peace and ease. Saltwater makes floating easier, it's also for teary days as tears complete the circle of life and blend into the water that holds us. The constant tides provide a balm that soothes weary hearts, bodies and minds and the sea swimmers hold space without being intrusive. Moments of awe and wonder in nature instills humility, acts of kindness and support by others are daily not occasional happenings. Jumping into waves of cold water in numbers lifts the heart, even on a miserable morning. I hope to be one of the post swim wrapped up tea drinkers right through this winter. I appreciate the value Youghal Sea Swimmers has within the Community. I hope it continues to be a powerful influence in the lives of so many people and a welcoming and inclusive community.

I am facing into my second winter of sea swimming. Still learning and practising, benefitting from Billy Carr's shared wisdom and encouragement. I now swim longer distances as part of an enthusiastic group of sea lovers in addition to my daily dip and have completed my first 750m swim as part of a relay team. I'll continue to build on endurance and distance and love it.

Martina Hooley

HOOKED

Never thought that I would do it,
No thanks. It's not for me!
That was before I did it,
Now the water has "hooked" me.

June '21 was when I started,
"The COVID" drove me mad,
I've to get out and meet some folk
Restrictions had made me sad.

When visiting my mother
She lives near Youghal you see,
She'd taken to the water
Loved it... And it was free!

So wanting to keep her company
I joined her, just us two
And then one day we heard about
A group "Please join us, do!"

Just needed togs and towel
And then the shoes and a hat
Dry robes and boots soon followed
But some don't bother with all that!

So that was how we started
And still going strong today,
All through the freezing winter
Until the waves heated up in May.

So no matter how I am feeling
Happy, stressed, or sad
It is always good to get in the water
Feeling that alive, can't be bad.

It's hard to be sad when you're jumping
Through a wild and sea weedy sea,
When you've got a group in there with you.
You feel happy, you're buzzing, you're free!

So thank you Youghal Sea Swimmers.
Thanks for your friendship all year.
I'm glad that my mum and I met you...
Now where is my bucket of gear?

Caroline Duffy

OPEN LETTER TO THE SEA

Dear Sea,

I am writing to you to express my gratitude that we are reunited. That we are finding joy in each other's company once more. When you claimed the life of my lovely friend over a decade ago, I became fearful of you, in a way I had never been before. I still tried but the joy and the fun were missing.

But they do say that every cloud has a silver lining. My cloud was the pandemic, my silver lining, a sea swimmer's group. Little did they know on that first day the trepidation I was feeling, the sense of loss reawakened, but only briefly.

The swimmers screamed, laughed, splashed and acted with sheer abandon. Before long, so did I. I was back in your foamy, sometimes gentle, sometimes wild arms and it felt so good!

In place of an underlying fear, came a new found respect. There are days I know I need to be more careful when I dive into your arms and days when I won't allow you to embrace me at all. You are just not in the mood! But most days you are there, waiting for me, calling me. Trepidation turns to thrill. Expectation turns to exhilaration. Fear turns to fun as I frolic in your waves. I feel a freedom to be childlike, to scream with abandon!

Every day I am so grateful for this new found joy, for this new sense of community, for this sense of belonging.

Thank you dear Sea,

Jo Breslin

Fenit Co. Kerry.
My first home and where my love of the sea began.

GROUP SWIM – REFLECTION

We gather; all shapes and sizes of us,
Some super-equipped and others with nothing but togs.
Mainly women, but some brave men do join us.
There is no glamour to this.
Plastic buckets for wet gear,
Supermarket shopping-bags, hair unbrushed,
Faces bare – maybe some sunscreen.
We huddle and chatter till someone makes a break for it
And we all follow.
Our white, goose-pimpled bodies invisible.
The odd comment on someone's nice swimsuit.
This is a place of acceptance and power.
We enter the water.
There are screams, squeals and silences.
Some of us get down as fast as we can,
Preferring our pain fast rather than anticipated.
Others take longer, waiting until the last… possible… moment.
The water is COLD.
But wonderful.
And we bob and float and chat and laugh.
Occasionally, someone swims a few strokes to warm up.
We share advice – "the booties are a game-changer" –
Where to get the best dryrobes.
How to manage your freezing toes.
The stresses and strains of the day or week wash away.
The cold sharpens the mind.
The sea welcomes all, as do its swimmers.
This is true privilege.
Eventually, reluctantly, someone admits to being cold.
We leave the water in ones, twos, groups;
The chatter – not just our teeth! – continues as we dress.
Some heading to work, others home to the shower.
See you next time!

Tracey Kennedy

MY SEA SWIMMING JOURNEY

I have lately been converted to sea swimming, finding it to be the most enjoyable activity I have ever undertaken in my lifetime. The exhilaration, joy and health benefits had escaped me from my childhood of the 1960s and the 1970s. This was perhaps because of the three-month custom of only swimming in June, July and August, put in place by my parents, no doubt with the best of intentions. As a child, I never questioned this custom, which was probably put in place by their parents before them. I suspect it was linked to safety concerns and a deep respect for the sea, which my parents loved.

After spending most of my life next to the water, it's no surprise that the ocean holds a special place in my heart. One of my favourite pastimes has always been to walk by the seashore with my dogs. I love the smell, the sound and the immense beauty of the sea. It never fails to evoke feelings of peace and tranquility, joy and elation, all at the same time. What I never realised was that immersion and swimming in the sea would enhance these wonderful feelings a thousandfold.

My earliest memory of sea swimming is as a toddler in Greenhole Strand, Youghal, holding the hand of my father as he swam with me in the clear blue water. I have wonderful memories of feeling safe and secure and afterwards eating jam sandwiches with red lemonade on the strand. In the 1960s, many people swam in Greenhole. People had a very deep respect for the sea. Unfortunately, I recall certain tragedies, but not in Greenhole, which is currently deemed too unsafe for sea swimming.

As an older child, I remember spending most of those long hot summers on the strand with friends, swimming to our hearts content. We children of the 1960s had such freedom to play, having fun, doing as we pleased, a freedom my own children unfortunately never experienced at this age. Before I headed out the strand on a beautiful summer's day, my father would always remind me not to go in the sea any further than my knees. These were promises which he and I both knew would not be kept. Nevertheless, this cautionary advice instilled in me a deep, healthy respect for the sea.

Moving on to teenage years, most of us kids still loved to swim in the sea. I have memories of cycling to Ardmore, Whiting Bay and Monatrae with our togs and towels and a picnic. Such wonderful memories of a bygone era.

Next came our working years, summer holidays and lovely memories of swimming in foreign shores, but alas no more swimming in the beautiful seas off the Irish coast, years and years of loving the sea but never again entering the life enhancing waters.

Many years go by and COVID-19 strikes. Fear, isolation and uncertainty are the order of the day. I realise how lucky I am that I can see and smell the sea and walk on its shores and meet and talk to people at a distance. Summer came and though restrictions continued, people could walk on the beach and swim in the sea providing they were living within the 5 km limit. I loved to walk across the sands and to meet people outside my little family circle.

Winter arrived and restrictions remained. I saw there were people who continued to sea swim. I was in awe and definitely curious. They continued to swim even on freezing cold days in the rain. No matter the weather conditions, they swam. There was I, wrapped in my warm winter woollies, thinking that I could never do that. I thought they must have been slightly insane. Nonetheless, I was full of admiration.

Summer days arrived again and one of my close friends suggested a swim in the sea. I will never forget that beautiful sunny July day in Pilmore as the three of us entered the freezing cold water. My first time in nearly 40 years! I could feel my heart pounding and as I gasped for air, I thought I would surely have a heart attack. I thought this would be the first and last time, but no, we went back again and again and again. We then began to go where people could see us. I even began to go alone if my friends were busy.

Eventually, I joined the wonderful group, known now as, "The Sea Swimmers". Winter came, I swam in the rain, the hailstones, the sub-zero temperatures. I swam at sunrise, at sunset, with the light of the moon. I even swam in the pitch black under the stars.

I am never as happy as when I am inside in that magnificent sea. It gives me a total affinity with nature. I am no longer just an inhabitant of the world, I feel part of this world. The power of the sea forces me to focus on the beauty of this earth, to be in the present moment and to leave all other thoughts and feelings behind. It makes me appreciate who and what I have in my life.

It is surely the nearest thing to heaven on earth, as all things worldly are left behind. It makes me appreciate the wonders of nature and how lucky I am to be in this moment.

It gives me an appreciation of my lovely friends and of my new-found sea swimming community. They are a remarkable group of amazing people and I thank them from the bottom of my heart.

Úna O'Neill Byron

THEY ARE OBSESSED

I can't meet you until after my swim. Oh, the buzz! You don't realise what you are missing out on.

It really activates the endorphins. It's really good for your headspace.

I heard all the clichés, I actually felt sorry for them because I thought THEY were obsessed, even addicted.

Then the tempting encouragement. You should try it; it would be good for your back (suffer from back ache).

No thank you! I remember as a child, shivering, teeth chattering as we got dressed, or in the days pre suntan cream pulling our t-shirts over sunburnt backs. Later, when I took my own children to the beach it appeared as if we were the chief collectors of sand, it was everywhere, between their toes, in their eyes, hair, clothes, towels and shoes. Oh, what a chore!

I have lived beside the beach for over sixty years and wouldn't even swim whilst abroad so why start now? Eventually after months of listening to a growing majority I decided to suss it out and see what THEY were raving about.

So, on a beautiful Saturday in May I crossed the bridge and headed to the Decies to a little beach that the locals refer to as the Curragbean. I had borrowed all the gear including the swimsuit, no point in investing in something that I wasn't going to commit to.

OMG, I picked a good day. It felt as if the sun had gobbled up the wind, there were gentle rolling waves, so conditions were ideal for my first splash. Afterwards Alice, Elaine, Michelle, Cora and I dined like queens in Alice's red camper. We relaxed with a coffee and croissants and as I looked back at the beach, I knew that I needed to start and do my own shopping.

I will always remember my first swim. Since then, I have met many lovely people through the Ballymermaids, The Curragh Swimmers, The Redbarn Randomers and in more recent times The Youghal Sea Swimmers. And then THEY started again, "You must go for a full moon swim" Steady up now I thought that's a step too far.

By Thursday 11th August I decided I might as well give it a go. We met at 9.15pm and amidst much excited greetings we made our way down to the water and just as we were wondering would he come out at all the beautiful red ball of the Sturgeon moon appeared on the horizon. Oh, what a magical experience. As it grew darker the sky and the sea became one. The water was dotted with bodies and multi coloured hats and you could hear the chatter across the beach. I felt at one with my fellow swimmers, it was lovely to take a breath and dwell in the moment. It was awe inspiring to watch the shimmering path of light ripple across the water. To add to the moment, we were joined by a seal who bobbed around and also seemed to be enjoying the experience.

I have had many highlights in my swimming career so far and look forward to many more. I now have a motivation to get up in the morning

I am obsessed and I have now become part of THEY.

Rosarii O'Brien

WATER

The sanderlings land on shore, newcomers or returnees? They jostle and push forward, competitive as ever, taunting the little waves, coming in and coming out, but now the waves are gone and reduced to a creamy surf.

Those little chattering birds step forward expectantly, their little feet supporting their plump bellies on glistening stones. They enjoy the crystal sound of water over stones as their feet support their plump bellies. Stepping in and out, again and again, challenging and challenging, but the little waves win…the sanderlings accept defeat. But they are not defeated. Their little plump bellies declare otherwise. They soar and soar away and are gone... but to where? Yet another day they will try again.

I, the observer, like to dive in the waves. Enjoyable as thrashing, gasping, gulping among the waves is. A kind of stillness descends. I'm immersed in a sensory meditation in this immense blue. A cold grip initially, then velvet. I'm part of it. The whoosh of the waves caresses, engulfs, holds you tightly and clings possessively. You are captive. You submit to the engulfing, clinging, separating, ebbing and parting water. I belong.

But realism hits me suddenly and it's a strange feeling. I let the water flow over my fingers. I won't ever experience this water again. Like the wind, the ebb and the flow will reveal new water and this in turn will go on forever.

And now just like the sanderlings, I wait and I wait, swimming around and around. I wait again. I am patient. It will happen and it does…high above a cloud moves on to reveal the sun. My secret delight. A golden pathway forms and opens up …I swim and swim along the sunbeam imploring it not to disappear and it doesn't. It is my secret delight. A sparkling carpet, beckoning, capturing, leading me along, to a golden infinity.

Mary O'Callaghan (Claycastle)

A Sea of Grief and Love

When I'm in the sea the fire in my chest eases, for a brief time I can breathe, every wave reminds me I'm alive, I'm still here and I have to live on for him.

When your child dies a part of you goes with them, you are never the same. My little boy Fionn would be 15 months old now, I wonder what he would look like? What would his first word have been? What would his personality be like? They say times a healer but it's a slow process.

The sea numbs the pain, it takes me out of the darkness, I always submerge my head three times for Fionn, I pray, I talk to him, I sing 'You are my Sunshine', it's a connection, a place where I feel close to my son.

During the COVID pandemic pregnant health care workers had to finish work at 28 weeks gestation. With my free time I walked miles on Youghal beach for the next few weeks. At 32 weeks pregnant I began swimming in the sea. On one of my many beach walks I found a conch shell, I put this in Fionn's coffin on the day of his funeral.

After Fionn's death weeks passed, where I longed to be dead too. In September another bereaved mother in Killeagh took me under her wing, I firmly believe our sons are friends up there and they brought us together.

Michelle took me to the sea, one late September evening. At high tide we entered the waves at Youghal Front Strand. It felt like the first breath of air I had taken in weeks, for a moment the pain eased.

The sea holds me. I would give anything for things to be different but this is my life now. Fionn lives in love, he's there when I'm with my family, my friends, my people, he lives on in all the love we have for each other. My good friends Fiona and Amy kept me going into the sea over the winter months.

In January 2022 I joined the Youghal Sea Swimmers. I am so grateful to have this amazing group of people, to have safety in the sea, to have the chats, to laugh together, to let out a shriek as we enter the sea together. On the darkest of days family, friends and the sea have kept me going and I know there are brighter days ahead.

Teresa Berkery

EBB AND FLOW

The soft wet sand
Underneath your feet
Walk to where
Tide and shore meet.

A cold wave that
Stops to crash and
Eases the ache
In one blue splash.

Tell the salty sea
Your worries and woes
Watch the tide take them
As it ebbs and flows.

As the white froth moves
And you lie beneath
Your chaos is calm
And the heart, it beats.

Aisling Curran

AN EARLY MORNING DIP TO START THE DAY.

I arrived at Youghal Garda station in early January 1999. I became the Community Garda in November 2009. I remember in my early years in Youghal, seeing a small number of hardy souls carrying their towels up Lighthouse Hill nearly every day, even in the winter. I remember meeting one of these daily dippers in her house in McCurtainstown. I was flabbergasted when she told me her age. I said to myself, "there's something in this sea swimming." I wasn't instantly converted, but it was something that used to play on my mind.

On New Year's Day, 2018, I decided to quit alcohol as a way of living a healthier life. It's a decision I'm delighted I made and have stuck to. On the 31st of December 2018, I made another decision. I googled the benefits and tips for all year round sea swimming. The advice was to bring a hot drink and don't stay more than five minutes in the water. I lived in Abbeyside at the time. On a cold, crisp, sunny day, I headed off to Abbeyside beach with my towel and flask of tea. I walked into the clear blue water. It was baltic. I splashed around for about three minutes. I got out, dried off and drank my tea. I felt brilliant and was instantly hooked. Bar a dose of flu, a bout of COVID and about four or five bad storms, I haven't missed a day since that first dip nearly five years ago. My favourite swimming spot is the castle end of Clonea Strand. I like nothing better than an early morning dip to start the day. I can't really explain the health benefits but it's a great way to feel alive. While I enjoy a nice dip in the Mediterranean when on holidays, it doesn't compare to the adrenaline rush of splashing around the Atlantic Ocean in January.

Peter Queally

Community Garda, Youghal.

Comforting Magic

I wake dreaming of being in it, the draw of it is strong. Tough days, sad thoughts, body aches all need soothing. Calling me, I know it will relax my mind and body, although not the only reasons, the thought of it is never far from my mind. When I wake, I am usually thinking; is there time available today, or a reason to celebrate or reward myself with this indulgence of energising magic? Frantic calculation checking the schedule of life's commitments that day, the forecast, traffic and responsibilities ahead, can I accept this magnetic pull? When I find a way, a gap, yes, I can, with a juggle and a jump up, I prepare what's needed, a simple kit of essentials for this incredible resource of healing. I'm in the car, excited and the magnetism does the rest and guides me to it.

The excitement of arriving and exiting the car, standing for a moment to absorb the smell, sounds and sights of this powerful entity that never looks the same in any moment, an ever-changing beauty of nature. The friendly smiles of others also preparing to venture in, combined with curious looks of disbelief from walkers bewildered at what we are doing, all bring such joy inside and amplifies the enthusiasm of my already bursting anticipation. Stripped down to just a swimsuit and a hat or booties in the winter months.

I am ready. Walking towards it, feeling the power at my feet with the first toe dip and then wading into its depths embracing its invigorating cold and rejoicing shock, grimacing, smiling, waiting to get deep enough to submerge. A deep breath in, I dive under, eyes open in my goggles, I feel home, awake, alive like nowhere else can imitate. A few strokes, keeping limbs moving to warm up, then I raise my head to the surface air again, my senses exploding with joy and life. Checking I am still in my depth with my feet touching the glorious sand below, limbs moving, body smiling, I look to the shore, then out to the horizon and absorb the atmosphere of the moment and then head off to swim some strokes, up for air as I need it, never allowing myself to get out of puff or stray too far away from others.

Looking to the shoreline to ensure I swim parallel and see where I left my bag and adapt to the tides as it brings me where it wants or at times nowhere, sometimes accelerating me forward other times being nature's swimming treadmill. Always aware, smiling inside and out. If there were worries, they are washed away for those moments with the sea. If there were aches, body or soul, they are pacified by this powerful body of comforting magic. After a few minutes in, the body is warm and can't get enough, staying, playing, jumping waves if they are there, swimming between them and diving under. When it is calm, having an occasional lie down, floating effortlessly looking up at the sky, caressed by its power.

Time passes and I must look at my watch and see who is still around, hoping it's not time to leave. Hurray! I can stay, there is still time for now, time to stock up on more joy. Eventually it's time to leave, the task of getting dry and clothed but bursting with adrenaline, looking around at others, all exalted with the joy this brings. Some stay for a hot drink or head off back to our busy lives, but now with the advantage this gives us to help us get through whatever life throws. I never regret a sea swim, the elation and soothing. It stays with me long afterwards and keeps me longing to return, again and again.

Lisa Stacey-James

SWIMMING WITH FRIENDS

Everywhere I go, I go for a swim. I make a point of swimming in as many different spots as possible. The Mediterranean, the Atlantic, the Indian and the Pacific and hundreds of beaches in between. Yet, the Divings in Youghal, opposite my home, remains the most wonderful place to swim. I bring my children, grandchildren, nieces and nephews to swim here regularly. Recently, I've had the pleasure of introducing my fellow sea swimmers to the spot.

Summer 2005. It is still and quiet, save for the odd car that passes on the Lighthouse Hill above. The air is heavy with the fresh smell of the seaweed. In the distance I can feel a faint heat from the rising sun, as it illuminates East Point and fills the sky with a palette of oranges and pinks. This is reflected on the sea and runs shimmering all the way to the horizon.

Having swam here all my life, I know where and when to enter the water. To the uninitiated, bed rock lurks below the water and may cause painful grazes and bruises. For an old hand, there are a number of pathways that are clear of low lying rock and allow for the deeper water to be easily accessed. Today, there is a high tide and I can let myself gently fall into the fresh morning tide. The initial bite of the cold quickly gives way to the comforting sensation of the water and my skin becoming acquainted.

There is a wonderful silence that is slowly broken by the distant puttering of a fishing punt on the far side of the river Blackwater's mouth. I begin my daily swim, on my back I paddle out towards the horizon looking back at the lighthouse that looms above. I allow the sea water do its invigorating magic; it is restorative and enlivening. It clears the head, as they say. The only way for a day to be started.

Suddenly, I'm interrupted. The water breaks less than ten yards away from where I tread water. Not one or two but four dolphins breach the water, one after another. Their breath heaves; loudly exhaling and gulping the air in and out of their blowholes.

As the water is clear and they approach me, I can make out the silhouette of these large and improbably graceful creatures. They are close enough for me to see the metallic blue of their fins and brilliant white bellies. They breach, sometimes in pairs, once in unison. All four dolphins declaring their presence!

For a few moments, I feel them acknowledge me. We are both just doing what we do every day in the water; like old friends. There is the sense of a moment in time in which we share this tiny part of the Atlantic Ocean together; circling a few times as if to bid me farewell, they disappear in the direction of Capel Island.

This moment reminds me how eternally lucky we are to have such a wonderful beach at our front door. We have a relationship with the ocean and nature that only those who live close to the sea can understand. Indeed, these last few years, there have been many moments that remind me of how fortunate I am. The support, camaraderie and memories we create by coming together as friends for a simple dip in the sea remind me of the time I swam with the dolphins in the Divings, under the lighthouse: an indelible experience of friendship that is to be forever cherished.

Liam Cooper

CHOICES...

Life Is A Series Of Choices, As You Choose So You Become...

Choices shape our lives and define who we are. Taking up sea swimming, a choice I never expected to make, connected me with others and brought unexpected blessings and personal growth. A choice often premised by others with the words 'insanity' or 'madness' that anyone would willingly choose to immerse oneself in freezing cold water.

Life is so much like the sea, often calm and serene, other times unpredictable and tumultuous. Sea swimming, like life, can also bring unexpected challenges. How we deal with those unexpected waves / challenges can teach us so much about how we can deal with life or sea. Always knowing, just as a wave eventually subsides and calm waters return, we too can weather life's storms and find calm once again.

I feel a great sense of joy swimming in our wild Atlantic Ocean, the feeling as each hand gently enters the water ahead of me barely disturbing the surface, watching the ever-changing seabed as I move over it and gaze at the horizon slowly changing in the distance.

It's hard to put into words, the thrill of diving, especially into high rolling waves. As the wave crashes overhead, I can sense the turmoil on the surface, I can see the water churning above while the calm water below envelops me as if I'm in a different world. The palpable energy from the passing wave stays with me as I slowly rise back to the surface, knowing that another wave could be on the way and I'll be ready.

When I float I often go into a meditative state, trusting the sea to hold me in its embrace, watching with awe the sky above, sensing the rise and fall of my body in the water, feeling the subtle changes in the air and water against my body, listening to muffled sounds off in the distance. And not too often, having my tranquility rudely disturbed by a wave crashing over me which normally elicits a squeal of laughter.

The biggest challenge I faced in sea swimming, was overcoming the fear of the cold and embracing that cold. It's been such a transformative experience offering me significant physical and mental health benefits. It does get easier, in time. As the body adjusts, so too does the mind. The cold embrace of the sea is invigorating and empowering.

I've developed a positive relationship with cold water. Some of the strategies I employed included gradually exposing myself to colder temperatures, focusing on slow controlled breathing techniques to calm the mind, allowing my body time to acclimatise to the cold and adding an element of fun and excitement to every swim, despite that often bracing cold.

Consistency and repetition are key to building up tolerance and developing a sense of comfort and enjoyment in cold water. The sea is formidable, It was very important for me that I developed the confidence and skills to enable me to access sea conditions before entering the water so every time I could ensure my swim ended safely with a smile on my face.

The overriding element that helped me to continue my sea swimming journey was finding a community of cold water swimmers.
That community is based in Youghal.

"Happiness is not by chance, but by choice". Jim Rohn

Catherine Davis

MOLL GOGGIN'S CORNER

I often think of Moll
As I turn to round the corner.

How she wailed in wait for the no-show ship
Skippered by her love.

Her heart, a martyr;
Holding on - hopeless.

All along the beach,
There are more who mourn in silence;

But they know that the sea and sand
Has a hand in the healing.

None seek solutions, but solace;
Somewhere in the ruins of the ancient forest.

Still, I picture Moll there,
Still waiting in despair.

Her gaze fixed upon the waves.
Her light drowned behind the tears.

Eoin Coyne

A MAGICAL SWIM SPOT

My swimming days began on the beach in nearby Ardmore. Some of my fondest childhood memories were the days when my mam would pick us up from school and instead of heading home, she would say we are off to the beach. Mam made it her priority that all four of us knew how to swim and so began a love of the sea, the beach and all that being near the water encompasses. I lived in cities for over a decade and was many miles from a beach until one day I decided to bid on an old lighthouse keeper's house, here in Youghal. That decision to bid on and luckily, take ownership of such a seafaring building has changed the course and direction of my life and further deepened my love for the sea.

In 2020, I found out we were expecting our first baby and like many new mothers, the main focus was on the birth (in hindsight, I wish I had known that it's such a tiny part of the journey) but it's actually what brought me back to the sea here in Youghal and to daily sea swims. I was so petrified about the birth that I decided that gritting my teeth and submerging myself into the winterish Irish Sea would allow me to realise my own strength and really appreciate the value of my own breath and its power too.

Turns out, I loved those daily dips and my sister jokes that I was actually cheating as the bump was like a little hot water bottle and maybe it was. It turned out that the preparation did really help on the day little Méasaí decided to arrive into the world. Our little girl now loves the sea too and shrieks with excitement when her little toes hit the white sands of Youghal beach.

I hope to continue this love for the sea that my mam instilled in me, in our little girl and hopefully in the generations to follow her too.

To me, the sea reminds us that everything in life comes and goes. Everything changes. Life goes on despite the ups and downs that inevitably cross our paths. It's that moment when the cold water hits the curve on your spine, you gasp for breath and you leave all your worries right there in the sea.

How lucky are we to have such magical swim spots right here on our doorstep?

Saoirse Fitzgerald

Granny Doesn't Knit

November 2022

My teenage grandchildren ask as usual what I'd like for Christmas.
No hesitation on my part. I know exactly what I want: thermal gloves and boots for sea swimming, please and maybe – from their parents -a dry robe.
Disbelief. Scepticism. Eye-rolling.

I also know exactly what they're thinking: "Other kids' grannies are at home, knitting beside the fire, or baking cakes for us, or just watching Corrie on the telly."
Your granny doesn't knit, kids, sorry.
She swims in the ocean with friends, with the dog – even, if it's August and 80 degrees – with a reluctant husband.

Granny and friends have fun. We shriek, we laugh, we jump through the breakers, we have coffee afterwards, we gossip. All's made right with the world.

Then my adult son unwisely, sarcastically, suggests I might need a wetsuit as well. "Wet suits are for wimps", I say gleefully, knowing that, as a keen kayaker, he always wears a wetsuit and goggles and helmet, gloves and boots.

Christmas Day, 2022

Under the tree, in a box with my name on it, are gloves, boots and a dry robe. And a pair of knitting needles.

Jean Kelly

LOVE YE ALL

Myself and Pat joined the sea swimmers' group two years ago in March. Since then, we have made so many nice friends. Every morning we are met with a smile, a hug and of course a cuppa.

Myself and Pat went through a tough couple of years with Pat's cancer. Sea swimming has changed our lives mentally and physically. It gave us a chance to forget our problems and to have a laugh! When we arrive all we hear is laughter and of course screams from Marguerite. After our swim we have a cuppa, a chat and of course some of Christine's beautiful baking!

Our world has changed for the better, getting the text in the morning, knowing our friends will be waiting. Myself and Pat have made friends for life. Thank you for inviting us to join this group of wonderful, brave, sea swimmers.
Love ye all.

Annemarie & Pat McGrath

In the womb of the waves
She soothes me.
Free from anger, fear, anxiety and gloom
She soothes me.
Quietens my troubled mind
Like a deep meditation.
Every time
In the womb of the waves
Mother ocean
She soothes me.

Mairéad Robinson

The tides come and go
Back and forth too and fro
The sun on the water
The sand between our toes,
The angry water tossing us about
The calm waters enveloping us with love.

Angela Tallon

SEA-ING IT FOR MYSELF...

I walk on the beach gazing into the sea, feeling numb. My body and mind in shock at the news I had just received. My dear friend had passed away suddenly, aged 43.

Thirty minutes earlier that December night, I ran out the front door away from my husband, children, home, running... to escape my new reality. Breathing the cold fresh air into my lungs helped numb my body. I didn't know where I was running to, but I put one foot in front of the other because my body and mind could not be still.

My destination was no longer my choice when the devastating news had reached another friend, she phoned me and picked me up. As her weighted passenger, I listened to her shock, her deep condolences and sorrow for my loss, our loss. The car came to a standstill at a dark, deserted Youghal prom. I can't remember if it was asked or offered. We both exited the car for a sea breeze walk. I don't remember what words were spoken. My mind was not my usual aid, I wanted to jump into the water to escape my thoughts, I wanted to leave my body and my alien mind.

I didn't jump in, because in my mind back then, only a crazy person would go into the water in December. On her first anniversary I woke up at 6am and went to the beach by myself to sit and watch the sunrise before work.

I didn't know why, but it helped me. I felt heartbroken, lonely, angry. Those feelings came, presented themselves and passed.

Drinking my coffee, breathing in the sharp fresh breeze, I felt privileged to be alive when my dear friend was not.

The year that followed brought about many changes in my life which often left me feeling lost. Change is scary but there's no growth in familiarity. So when it was suggested to me to have a dip in the sea I reluctantly decided to try it. I had not been in the sea since I was a teenager. The previous year I would not have considered putting on a swimsuit at my local beach but with loss comes the realisation that life is very short, so I thought I'd try it out, just once.

My neighbour introduced me to the group that I had seen many a morning running into the sea. I always thought "those people are crazy!"

Now, here I was, joining the crazy people. Me, a non-swimmer, a non-believer, dipping in the cold Youghal sea in April, not a wetsuit in sight. I took a deep inhale when the water hit my feet. As it hit the more delicate parts of my body I screamed!

It was freezing cold! But the warmth I felt radiating from this group was incredible. Not a hot tub or a wetsuit in the world could compare! I was converted. The energy I feel at the beach provides me with comfort. It's not just the calming sound of the breaking waves or the children playing in the sand or the dogs enjoying the freedom of the open space, nor is it the smiling faces of strangers and locals giving and receiving passing friendly glances.

I now love the cold water hitting my body. The waves crashing against my skin. The loud screams and laughter from my sea buddies.

Most of all the hugs and chats and love radiating from my crazy people.

Tara

Swimmers by
Bobby Klang

TRIATHLON - WHAT A FEELING!

Ironman came to Youghal in 2019 and OMG was I in awe of all the competitors. I made a pact with my friend Claire that we would enter the next Ironman in Youghal! First task is to accomplish a 3.8K sea swim – not going to be easy considering I have a fear of putting my head underwater! On top of that, trying to navigate around stinging jellyfish, freezing cold water, bad weather, foggy goggles, swim shoes, gloves etc. After a while I gained confidence and managed to swim 1.5KM – but still had self-doubt on how I could keep going to 3.8KM. Sheer determination, motivation and self-belief and huge support from family and friends, I made it to 3.8KM. What a feeling to go from 0 to 3.8KM of sea swimming – those three years of training paid off! Fast forward to Ironman Youghal on Sunday 14th August 2022. I stood at the start line feeling a little overwhelmed and nervous but I used the nervous energy to spur me on.

Next thing I knew I was in the sea – despite plenty of elbows landing my way and some pushing and shoving, all my hard work paid off. I found my stride and got into a nice rhythm and never looked back. Next thing I realised I was out of the sea and rounding the corner of Moll Goggins. What a view! Just a sea of people lining the pier clapping and cheering all of the competitors just like I did back in 2019, it was the best feeling ever! I couldn't believe that I fulfilled my dream of competing in the Ironman Youghal, just like the competitors I was in awe of back in 2019. All my hard work and frustration was replaced with a feeling of huge accomplishment and pride in myself.

Carol Murphy

A PLACE CLOSE TO OUR HEARTS

During the summer holidays in the 1970's the beach was our playground. We had great freedom and many hours were spent in the company of friends swimming or playing games on the beach. A popular spot for us to meet up was where the sea swimmers now meet. Most of us learned to swim using tubes or arm bands, we had no formal swimming lessons. There were no 'dry robes' and many of us were left shivering after spending too much time in the sea in all kinds of weather.

Aside from swimming, the beach was also used for various other types of games. When the tide was out, there were regular soccer games held at the beach as it provided a perfect surface for the game. Local derbies between boys from the strand and the town were very competitive contests. Games like tennis and hop scotch were played with lines drawn in the sand used as guides for the game. We also had skimming stone contests with numerous efforts being made to get the biggest number of bounces.

Rockpool fishing and catching crabs was also a favourite pastime with the rock pools in front of the Strand Palace being a great place to spend hours seeing various forms of sea life.

Perks were also located at 'The Gap' which was an added attraction with outdoor slide, bumpers, ghost train, slot machines and various other rides being some of the main highlights. Loudspeakers provided music by singers such as Joe Dolan's 'Make me an Island', Tom Jones 'It's Not Unusual' and Elvis 'If I could Dream' which all added to the atmosphere.

Fifty years later, it is great to see a group still swimming in the same popular spot on Youghal Beach. A place close to our hearts.

Martina O'Halloran (Smiddy)

THE SPLASH

A late Saturday night in July, checking the forecast, checking the tide times, should I make food for tomorrow, no, that's tempting fate!!

Sun rises early, rays streaming in my back window, Yes, it's on!,

Pancakes & orange juice for breakfast, that'll do me for the day.

Pack the bag - apple, Taytos, bit of chocolate, water bottle, towel, mat, book, headphones. Life is better in flip flops...

Togs on at home or change at the beach? To cycle or to walk ? Walking means a 99 on the way out, cycling means a 99 at the beach... hmmmm...

Finally, on the way, hello to all the locals out walking on Lighthouse Hill, 'yes, I'm heading out for the day'

Past the lighthouse, then Moll Goggin's, heart racing and there it is, the sparkling sea, the Front Strand and remembering that every Youghal person who goes to Bondi beach says 'is that it, like?!!'

Find a spot near the Lifeguards, settle myself in and then into the water - THE SPLASH, straight down and stay down. Let the water hold you.

Tara McCarthy

SALTWATER BLESSING

for Anne, my mother

I never knew when it was coming.
Following her own inner tides,
My mother would appear at the bedroom door,
A small bottle of Medjugorje oil nestled snugly in her palm.
Leaning down, eyes closed, she would murmur a blessing,
A sacred ritual, a beannacht, seeking healing, protection.

She always said the sea is in our blood.
Coming from a small fishing village deep in West Cork,
She grew up salt-stained
With an intrinsic sense of our connection
to the beating blue heart of the wild Atlantic.
We came forth on a wave of water,
Our hearts beat in time with tides and currents,
Saltwater flows in our blood.

As we got older, I begged her to swim with me,
like she used to when I was a child,
"You don't realise I'm old – the cold could kill me!"
So I waded out alone, tentacles of seaweed unfurling around me
as the sea welcomed me in its icy embrace.
Looking back, I often spotted her hunkered on the shore,
Splashing her face with salt water.
Leaning down, eyes closed, murmuring a blessing.
A sacred ritual, a beannacht, seeking healing, protection.

Kelly Motherway

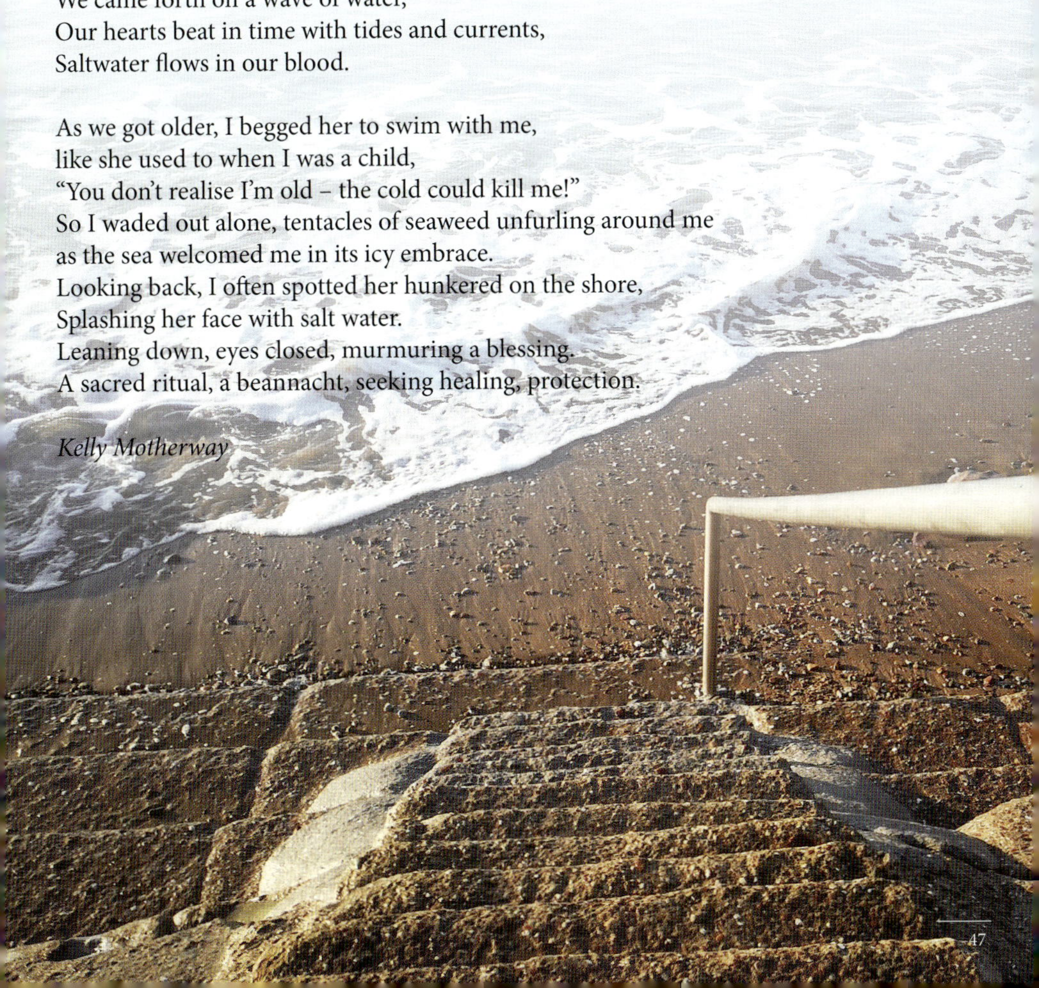

SOLSTICE

The sunshine glistens
On the water's edge
White horses dance
The waves come to fetch.

A circle of friends
Into the water we go
The tide it takes us
Into its soft flow.

A magic surrounds us
That we can't explain
A haven of blue
The sea keeps us sane.

Where once we were strangers
Now friends we've become
An ocean of kindness
Where all are welcome.

Aisling Curran

SEA SWIMMING -WASHING ALL MY WORRIES AWAY...

COVID has been an upheaval and an unwelcome visitor in my life, but it has given me and many others the gift of sea swimming. The cold water brings calm and a sense of achievement, which is good for the body and the soul. It creates a bond of warmth and sense of community among the dippers and swimmers.

All my senses are enhanced on a calm or windy day – hearing the sounds of the waves, the cry of the gulls, the laughter and shrieks of my fellow swimmers. Seeing the beauty and contrasting colours of the sky and the ocean and the smiles of those around me is uplifting. The salty taste of the water and the warmth of a shared cuppa is amazing. Breathing in the smell of the sea air is cleansing and calming as I plunge into the ocean and feel the pure sensation of the water washing all my worries away.

Sea swimming is the best gift I have ever received.

Josephine Morrissey

I LOVE TO WATCH THE WATER

My name is Daiva. I grew up in Lithuania. Swimming was always a popular sport in my country. I learned how to swim myself in the river called Nemunas when I was young. There was also a great selection of swimming pools in Lithuania.

I remember as a young girl going to the local swimming pool. I was told to come back when I could swim properly. So, I travelled to another pool which was far away from where I lived. I didn't tell my parents as they would not allow me to travel alone by bus to the pool. For one year I travelled to the pool to get swimming lessons with a coach. One day the coaches took me aside and told me that they saw potential in me and they wanted to enter me in long distance swimming competitions. However, they needed permission from my parents. I was very nervous as my parents still did not know that I was travelling to this pool across town by myself on the bus.

As my love for swimming superseded my nervousness, I decided to go to meet my mother after work to tell her. When she met me she instantly knew that something was wrong. I blurted out that the coach wanted to train me twice a day and prepare me for competition. She was angry at first but realised that I loved swimming and that the trainers saw potential in me. I was a teenager, so all my focus was on swimming. My parents gave me permission to participate in the coaching sessions, so every day I trained and improved. I was picked to represent my town in National Swimming Competitions. I was chosen to represent my country in long distance swimming competitions which I loved.

In summer, we competed in competitions at the lake when we were taken to a summer camp. In hindsight, I don't think that the lake was safe to swim in. We all swam with a knife attached to our leg. The knife would help me free myself when I got caught in the stubborn reeds and rushes in the lake. One day I was competing in a swimming competition in the lake and I got caught in the reeds. I got an awful fright which affected me. I became nervous which affected my swimming. I decided to give up swimming, but I still loved the water. When I moved to Youghal over twenty years ago I knew nobody. I had my little girl Mary who was young at the time. I was lonely so the only place that I found company was to walk by the sea with my buggy.

I still love the sea now. I don't swim anymore as I am nervous of the waves, but I love to walk by water. Water calms me. When I go on holidays on a cruise, I love to watch the water as it relaxes me.

Daiva

HELEN HERLIHY (OUR LEGEND)

In the fifties Mam left the tide in her birthplace, Tramore and came to Youghal. In the early days she did not swim much as she was too busy dancing in the Showboat. She got married in 1956 and had six children. We have wonderful memories of our days spent on the beach.

When we got older, she had two swims a day, sometimes three. She would shout over the garden fence to her neighbours Lydia and Francis "are we off girls?" She would head off down to the second breaker dressed in her gown, pearl earrings, headband and of course her bright red lipstick. No matter what the water was like, she would say it was "delicenfolder or gorgelious". Her motto was – if there was anything going on in anyone's life she would say "give it to the tide". It was her daily therapy and one of her favourite things to do.

One day there was a strong current which dragged her over to the pier. Luckily someone saw her and rescued her. When he asked her how she felt her answer was "shur boy there is no better way to go, you just float away".

She was famous in town for the Christmas Swim which she did every year until 2012, raising much needed funds for the Youghal Lions Club. She dressed up every year as Mrs Claus on Christmas Eve and sat inside the door of SuperValu, spoke to everyone that passed and had lollipops for the kids – they all loved her!

On Christmas Day she would be first into the tide – last out. We would all be frozen waiting for her to come out shouting "Gran" from the shoreline, but of course she only came when she was ready.

In 2013 her health had deteriorated and that Christmas she dressed in her swimming attire but she was not well enough to swim. That was the saddest day for all of us as we watched from the seafront.

Nowadays sea swimming is a popular thing to do with so many benefits. Years ago she often was the only one in the tide – people thought she was cracked. I guess she was ahead of her time and knew the secrets of the sea.

After her swim she always sat on no 8 seat which she claimed to be hers. She spoke to all the people who passed by but if someone did not say hello she would say "shur love what's wrong with them – it takes nothing to say hello"!

In her final years she would walk to the end of the prom – take a rest – that's where her plaque is today which says;

"Helen Herlihy, Our Legend,
I did it my way".

Every time we sit by her plaque we smile and feel her presence,
her positive attitude to life and all the wonderful memories we have.
She will always be our legend and our favourite swimmer in town.
We will always love you.

The Herlihy Family

KEVIN STACK

My brother Kevin Stack swam in the diving rocks in Youghal all his life. He started going to the diving rocks in 1964 and swam there ever since.

Though he lived in Enniscorty, Co, Wexford, he would arrive in Youghal at weekends, drop his gear and straight away head to the diving rocks. No matter where he went in the world nothing was better than the Divings in Youghal. We always knew where to find him. He was happiest down at the diving rocks.

MICHAEL WALSH

To remember Michael is to picture a man in a pink shirt, unbuttoned at the top and towel under his arm as he walked out to his beloved Youghal beach. In his early years he swam the 49 steps with Liam Burke and Martin Hallinan and the late Kevin Stack and Mikey Joyce to mention but a few. In his later years he became an exclusive member of the 'swimming group'. Many a laugh, discussion and debate they had in their spot out the "far off". Helen Stack, Mary Noonan and Cassie Moloney and the late Ann Foley and Eileen Hallinan used to tell him he was "blessed amongst women".

Derry O'Sullivan

Derry O'Sullivan was born in Browne Street, Youghal in The Anchor Bar in 1942. Aged 4 years, playing by the double slips, he fell in and managed to doggy paddle towards a rope and held on until help arrived! This is where his affinity for the sea began, but also aware of safety aspects, he often mentioned *"you must have a healthy respect for the sea"*.

He swam throughout the year with a likewise group of men – all daily swimmers – from the rocks beneath the lighthouse. They bought cement and recreated a structure enabling them to dive as past generations had enjoyed.

HOGAN TWINS

I have so many fond memories of Sean and his friends, as they formed a central part of our summers in Youghal. It was Sean who encouraged me to emulate my mother, Terry Aherne of Catherine Street, in taking on the ferry swim.

I was 15 in the summer of 1968 when Sean and I embarked on the swim. We entered the water midway between Green Hole and the lighthouse. The sea was calm and accompanying us in a rowing boat was Jim, Sean's twin, Mary, my sister and Mary McAuliffe (Horgan).

We swam towards Monatrea House. I still remember the sensation of my feet touching the ground when we were near the beach at Monatrea. We walked up onto the beach, by the wall of the house, joined by our boat crew. They had towels for us and a hot drink from a flask.

Then it was time for the return swim. We were aiming for the ferry slip. We hadn't told anyone of our plan for the swim, but as we were nearing the ferry slip, a small crowd had gathered and were applauding.

Sean was a vibrant presence during our Youghal summers, full of energy and brimming with enthusiasm. He did so much to promote swimming and life saving. He was a true standout character.

Patricia Martin

Our annual summer holidays in Youghal were always looked forward to with great joy, happiness and anticipation. Carefree days with family and friends, swimming, boating and walking.

Swimming was a daily activity. We walked out to the Front Strand, to 'our spot', joined by our Youghal friends. This was our daily joy.

It was a natural progression to join Sean Hogan's Life Saving Classes. Sean led 'Life Saving' instruction during the school summer holidays. We would gather for instructions at the ferry slip. We would have theory and land based life saving in the old Scout's Hall.

Sean gave so generously of his time.

Mary Martin

IN MEMORY OF
SEAN HOGAN
1947 – 1999
FOR HIS CONTRIBUTION TO
SWIMMING & LIFE SAVING

SWIMMING IN YOUGHAL THROUGH THE AGES

My grandfather Jim and his brothers Phil and Tom were photographers and filmmakers in the late 1800's and early 1900's. They took thousands of photographs of local events and scenes. The photograph below was taken in 1913. It is a family photograph of my grandfather, grandmother and other family members.

This photo would have been a bit risqué at the time. It wasn't really acceptable to be seen in your swimming attire, let alone being photographed in it. The brothers had a photographic studio in Friar Street and were once asked by the Parish priest to remove the photos of the beach from the shop window as they were considered to be indecent. Uncle Phil refused to take the photos down and told the Parish priest he need only go for a walk out the beach and he'd see the same thing any day of the week. The photos stayed up. This photo was taken on the Mall beach and 109 years later we have photographs of their grandchildren, great grandchildren and great-great grandchildren swimming in the same place.

The photo above was taken in the Horgan Brothers Photographic Studio on Friar Street where people could come and have their photo taken with props and backdrops such as the beach scene featured here.

THE SLOB BANK

People who lived around the Tallow Street area swam in the pool at the Slob Bank. This was a salt water pool that was filled by the tide as it went in and out. My Aunt's brother in law, Joe Slattery told me that a huge number of people swam there, men, women and children. The swimming tended to start in April and finish in September. He also told me that they learned to swim in the pool. When they were older they would jump off the sluice gates into the River Blackwater and swim down towards what were known locally as the "double slips", a small set of slipways at the shipping dock. One well-known local man would walk daily across the fields in his togs with a newspaper under his arm. He would climb into the pool and proceed to float on his back whilst reading the newspaper without ever getting a single page of the paper wet.

ROSALEEN CRONIN

Youghal had many colourful characters over the years. One of these was a lady named Rosaleen Cronin. Rosaleen was a powerful swimmer. Joe Slattery told me that she used to jump off the Sluice and swim across to Ferry Point and back, a journey not many would risk today. Moby Dick was filmed in Youghal in 1954. Rosaleen was very eager to get Gregory Peck's autograph which was almost impossible as the film crew had cordoned off the quay to prevent people from interfering with the filming. Rosaleen was not a lady to be easily deterred and climbed down the quay ladder, near where the pontoon is situated today. She swam around the corner with her autograph book and pen held up in one hand while using the other to propel herself towards Gregory Peck. All filming had to be stopped due to the intrusion but you can be sure Rosaleen got her autograph. Below are some photos of Gregory Peck taken during the filming of Moby Dick in Youghal.

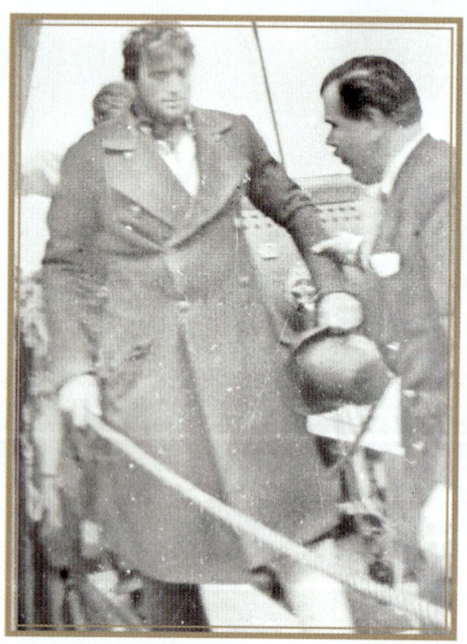

Summer to us living in the Mall and Strand Street was all about swimming. We lived for swimming. We were lucky enough to live at a time when there were large families and everyone swam. Aunts, uncles, neighbours all had endless free entertainment. I have a memory of being 3 years old and being very annoyed with my mother. The reason for this was because she put away the swimming things for the winter. At this age I couldn't see why she would do such a thing. I couldn't see any logic in it so I decided to take matters into my own hands. One day in October I decided to go for a swim. I sneaked into the kitchen and found my togs in a basket at the bottom of the hot press. I then took off out the gate, across the road and over to what was known as the Bailiff's slip. I put on my togs and proceeded to go down the slip to the water. The tide that day was out and therefore at its most dangerous. I was just about to put my foot in the water when my sister's friend Joan O'Keeffe who incidentally was only 7 or 8 years of age happened to come out the back gate of her house and ran down to stop me. The anticipation of that swim still stays with me, I will never forgive her. Thanks to Joan for probably saving my life but ruining my swim. Meanwhile, half the neighbourhood was out looking for me. My swimming addiction started early.

The second episode happened in Monatrea, across the harbour from our home in the Mall. A group of us children were brought across to the Ferry Point by boat and dropped in a safe place to swim. A parent was reading a book up on the beach and perhaps not paying the fullest of attention. Finding this a bit tame, we told them that we were going for a walk. We escaped and headed for the Ferry Point. We went to the southern end of the point where the current had become extremely strong. The idea was that we would swim out into the current which would then take us, right around the point to the northern side. Woosh! At the other side we would have to swim for our lives (literally) to make it back to shore on the other side. Who needs a water park? We did this seven or eight times until it was getting harder and harder to swim the distance back to the shore. At this stage we began to realise just how dangerous it was. Luckily, we never tried this trick again. Below is a photo of Ferry Point showing where we swam with the current.

The Ferry Slip

When I was about 10 or 11, we proceeded to learn lifesaving and water safety, at the Ferry Slip, by two men who did fantastic work for the community. They were twins, Seán and Jim Hogan. These were uncles of Linda Donoghue. They gave so much of their time to the young people of the town. For years we would go to the slip each summer and learn life saving techniques from them. We also did land drills and resuscitation, all of which was done on a voluntary basis by Seán and Jim. One particular year Seán and Jim were kind enough to bring us by ferryboat to Ferry Point for a picnic. This photo shows the ferryboat which ran regularly from Youghal Ferry Slip across to Monatrea.

The Mall Dock

Those who lived in Kent Street, on the far end of the Mall, swam in the Mall Dock or Cissy's Mall as we used to call it. Cissy was a lovely lady who looked after all the children that swam in the Mall dock. The Mall dock at the time was very different to what it is today and would have been home to several traditional fishing boats called Salmon Yawls which would have been moored there while not out at sea. When the mackerel came into the Mall Dock, sprats would come in ahead of them leading them into the enclosed area. Sometimes the fishermen would put a net across the dock to trap the fish. There would have been so many mackerel in the small area that children used to be able to swim in and pull them out of the water by hand. Their parents would have been delighted with a meal of fresh fish that evening. Sadly, in recent years the sight of shoals of mackerel arriving in the Mall Dock has become something of a distant memory.

THE MALL

My grandmother, May Horgan, who was seen in the first photo swimming with her husband and family, swam in the Mall every day from May to October. She would have her "dip" as she used to call it. She continued to do this every year until the age of 82, never deterred by cold water, jellyfish or shoals of mackerel. There used to be boats moored in the Mall so you could swim from one boat to the next, climb on board and perform your best bomb dive into the water. There were certain rites of passage that we went through. One was to swim out to the Bailiff's launch which was a boat owned by the Irish Fisheries used to patrol salmon poaching. This boat was the one moored furthest out from the shore, hence needing the greatest amount of strength and effort to reach it. If you could swim to the Bailiff's launch and back to shore you knew you had made it.

Another rite of passage was to jump off the quay wall. To this day you can see youngsters trying this while everyone in the quay holds their breath in anticipation. It could often take twenty minutes to finally get the courage to jump. The biggest challenge of all was the ferry swim which involved crossing the mouth of Youghal bay to Ferry Point in Waterford. This is a long distance across a stretch of water where tides could be difficult to row against, let alone swim. This was the greatest achievement for us as it had to be timed with great precision. Tides, winds and currents had to be just right. It was dependent on having someone to row a boat alongside you just in case you ran into difficulty in the deep water. The photo below is of the Mall and was taken in the late '40s to early '50s.

GREENHOLE

Many people swam in Greenhole, very few swim there now but it would have been very popular up to twenty or thirty years ago. I can vaguely remember that there were two bathing boxes at the side of Greenpark which were used by swimmers to get dressed before and after their swim.

THE DIVING ROCKS

The Divings, located below the Lighthouse, would always have been known as the "men's diving rocks" as it was only men who swam there. Thankfully that day is gone. For me, this is one of the nicest places in the town to swim. But like many swimming spots in Youghal the conditions must be just right to swim there. Full tide and not too much wind. The photograph here was taken around the 20s or 30s judging by the long sleeved, long legged togs worn. The sailing ship in the distance is the "Kathleen and May". As you can see, there was a diving board in place at the time. In more recent years it was taken away as it was deemed to be too dangerous. It must have been a fabulous sight to see these ships sailing out of the harbour while you took your swim from the diving rocks. Local fisherman Michael Coveney once told me a story. When Michael and his wife Biddy got married, they stayed in a flat under Pop Donovan's shop. Pop Donovan ran a sweet shop and petrol station just on the strand side of the Lighthouse which literally hung over the edge of the cliff, giving a fabulous view of the harbour and the Diving Rocks. Michael told me how he once looked out the window of the flat to see the swimmers enjoying themselves diving from the board at the diving rocks not realising that they were jumping into the water alongside two enormous Basking Sharks who were on the sea bed. While Basking Sharks aren't known to be dangerous, you could still imagine the fright you'd get if one of them, nearly the length of a bus crept up beside you.

Youghal Men Who Found Themselves Swimming in the Most Horrific of Circumstances.

My uncle, Paddy McGrath, was a member of the Merchant Navy during the Second World War when his ship was torpedoed. He told my mother the story of how he was thrown from the ship and left swimming in the middle of the ocean with not a sight of land for miles around. He said it was absolutely terrifying, like something from a nightmare. He was left swimming in the cold water with the rats that had escaped from the hold of the ship. Products for making Bovril on the ship were also floating around him. The crew were rescued this time but Paddy was left terrified after the ordeal. Nonetheless, he continued his career in the Merchant Navy and his next assignment involved sailing from New York on a ship called the Empire Heritage. This was a steam tanker which was carrying military equipment including Sherman tanks and trucks. Unfortunately for Paddy, for the second time in his life the ship he was travelling on was hit by a torpedo. This time on the 8th of September 1944 just north of Tory island, Paddy along with some other crew members managed to swim to safety and were eventually rescued by the crew of a ship called the Pinto. However, this ship was later targeted and it too sank. Paddy died only a relatively short distance from home after having been torpedoed three times. He was only 24 years of age.

I went to a talk in the Devonshire Arms Hotel about 25 years ago where I heard a local man Larry O'Sullivan speaking. Larry was a member of the O'Sullivan family who made ropes in a place locally known as the rope walk which is pictured below. The rope walk ran alongside the town walls in Youghal and you can see Larry pictured as a young boy helping his parents in the photo.

Larry told the story of how he was on board the ship H.M.S. Exeter when it was sunk in a battle with the Japanese in the Java sea. Larry and another Youghal man were left with no choice but to jump off the ship into shark infested waters. However, not to be discouraged by what must have been a terrifying experience. As the men jumped from the ship they could be heard shouting out "Moll Goggin's corner here we come". Larry was later picked up by the Japanese and sent to a prisoner of war camp and not only survived the camp but also the atomic bomb being dropped on Nagasaki. Miraculously, Larry did indeed survive to make it home to Moll Goggin's corner and it was fascinating to hear him recount the story as an elderly man many years later.

EXCURSIONS TO YOUGHAL

Every year, over four thousand children from parts of Cork city were brought to Youghal by rail on a special excursion to the seaside. This event, according to the Cork Examiner newspaper, was established around 1893 and was funded by Cork Businesses and a committee chaired by the Lord Mayor of Cork. It was sponsored by large Cork based businesses like Beamish & Crawford and Thompson's Bakery. A ladies committee provided food for the children such as sandwiches, cakes and sweets. Special trains were even provided for the occasion to carry the children from Cork to Youghal. My grandfather filmed the children coming off the train and you can almost feel the excitement as you see them running into the sea. This photograph was taken from the film, so the quality is not so good , but it gives an idea of the number of children arriving on the beach. Notably, on the right hand side of the photo, you can see the bathing boxes which would have been provided on Youghal beach to allow beachgoers to get dressed in comfort and privacy.

As you can tell from the stories above, life in Youghal has centred around swimming, diving, boating and fishing for generations and will no doubt continue for generations to come.

Patricia Whyte

An Original Sea Swimmer

As I type this, the mist is down, the drizzle constant and the wind getting up. So what's new about my Youghal experience this year compared to any other of the previous 65 years? It is simply the company of others swimming in the sea! I can talk of past times with the best of you about days gone by, dances in the Strand Palace, discos at Redbarn and The Hilltop Hotel. Visits to the merries, the trains coming down from Cork to the Front Strand on a Sunday for the day trippers, walking across the barrel bridge to pick up the bus on the other side in Co Waterford and many other misty-eyed memories captured in black and white photos.

We spent hours swimming and messing down the Front Strand, moving from our spot beside watchful parents to more grown-up gatherings towards Claycastle. Rarely year after year did we have many companions in the water. I should explain we were the English born children of Irish parents who came back to Youghal and holidayed here year after year. Many times we were described as 'mad'!

What Youghal means to me and what the sea has provided is constancy in an ever-changing world. The numerous challenges faced as we grew up, had families, health issues and various hardships, especially through the global pandemic of COVID, but to look up towards Redbarn, across to Knockadoon and over to Capel Island is soothingly always the same.

I feel anchored in this place. I am grateful for it and have loved sharing it.

Bernadette Barber (nee Walsh)

WADE

Giggles of excitement
Audible from the hidden cove
Feminine energy abundant
At this sacred dawn gathering.

No more camouflage
Nakedness marries nature.
You wade
Ankles to knees to thighs
You gasp
Goose pimpled skin, pert nipples
Submergence
Now your time to flirt
with the sea.

Tattooed bodies
Sun kissed skins
Maimed breasts
Body piercings
Us girlies similar in our individualities
Unique as the grains we tread.

Cold water creeps
Into body crevices
Breaststroke style
Into the frothy breakers
We embrace this wildness
Nourishing our souls.

We emerge
Shimmers of delight
Emerald fronds, bladderwrack
Draped on our flesh
Laughing now
We were brave
In our birthday attire.

Lizzy Doupe

INSPIRATIONS

Following an absence from sea swimming I took it up again at age 51 in July, 2021. The last time I swam I was 15 yrs old. I swam at Whiting Bay and Ardmore, Co Waterford. My fellow sea swimmers and Billy Carr have inspired and encouraged me. Through daily practise, my swimming has become stronger and my tolerance and love for the ice-cold salt water has become like an addiction. I cannot wait to join my fellow swimmers daily. The benefits are enormous and include noticeable improvement in my hair, tightening of my skin and I am frequently complimented on my glow. The mental benefits are most profound and include increased energy, tolerance, clear mindedness and increased enthusiasm and ability to solve all that life dishes out. I have read that swimming in the sea enhances blood circulation, reduces inflammation and I believe that the lymphatic system also improves.

Paddy Conaghan has been an ongoing inspiration as he travels Ireland raising funds and awareness for mental health charities. I have had the pleasure of sea swimming with Paddy on a number of occasions.

I invite you to seriously consider sea swimming. And, if at all possible, try and swim as the sun rises in the East and witness the reflected colours of the sunshine in the water as blues, pinks, golds, azure and diamonds dance in front of you.

Please put a date on your calendar and start. We advise always swimming with another person or several others. Never swim alone.

Tina

YOU ARE A SPECK IN THE OCEAN!

Swimming in the sea to me is an energy, a physical force and a spiritual event, depending on its mood! Once you enter this force you are wrapped in its calmness. As you look at the horizon and vast amount of water that surrounds you, you disappear in thought. You are a speck in the ocean, in God's infinite space. As you spread your worries across the water they dissolve. Memories come flooding in of loved ones who have passed, of happy and sad moments in life. I say a little prayer and reflect as the sun shines on the water creating sparkling diamonds that delicately dance on the surface. It brings a smile to my face and happy thoughts of my mum. You return to the shore feeling exhilarated, calm, lighter in worry and thoughts (cold!) but ready for what the day will bring.

Paula

FRONT STRAND AT SUNSET

"A thing of beauty is a joy forever", that's what comes to mind. It can be applied to many things. Sadly, I don't have Keat's gift of narrative or poetry.

Over the last few years since COVID, I discovered the Front Strand. That is to say for me I have found that I was walking on a magnificent thing of beauty. I have always enjoyed walking. I try to walk regularly and drink in the beauty around. Sometimes I have to pinch myself when I am strolling on the prom. The rolling waves excite me and I just have to stop and ponder the wild beauty of the roaring sounds crashing at me. When the tide is out I feel comforted and safe. Sometimes I am attracted to go out. As I head out westward towards the sun in the late afternoon I am struck at what beholds me. A vast expanse of golden sand being gathered up by the fast sinking sun. I have to stop and take a shot with my phone/camera, not that I fancy myself a photographer.

It's so overwhelmingly beautiful. I know I can keep it in my inner eye in case my photo isn't on. Before me a sky, alight with shades of vermillion, orange, yellow framed in a soft blue sky. The ball of yellow is sinking. I am rooted to the sand. I don't recall how long I stood there drinking it in – I'll be back!

Úna Furey

HOW DID I BECOME A SEA SWIMMER?

I always liked swimming in open waters. Back home in Bavaria it would be in rivers and lakes, mainly during holidays. Since living in Youghal with our wonderful beaches I took to the sea with pleasure - maybe from June to September, a rare dip in October and only if the weather was at its best.

What changed is that I became a dedicated 'sea swimmer' who embraces a dive almost every day summer and winter. Was it the dreaded COVID which confined us so much? Some of us met casually during summer, in the afternoons, or when the tide was right. We enjoyed the company and swimming together, so Linda decided to start an app to let us know who would be around and when. Nobody in their wildest dreams could have envisaged what happened - it grew from 6 to almost 300 within 3 years.

Suddenly everyone interested could put down a time and people joined - from as early as 6.30am in the morning to all hours in the evening. We started to organise social events around the swim - a moonlight swim, a sunrise swim, a Halloween swim, solstice celebrations, always accompanied by lanterns, music, flasks and home baking and most importantly by fun and laughter. I met people I never knew before and got to know others whom I might have just known briefly and great friendships formed.

What happened when the days got shorter and cooler? We just kept going! Suddenly these huge black coats called dry robes appeared which made you look like a big crow. We wouldn't buy nice clothes anymore (where would you go during COVID) but plastic shoes, swim hats and gloves, towelling robes and swimsuits. Swimmers joined us from all surrounding areas, Tallow, Ballymacoda, Killeagh, Midleton, just to name a few places. Marguerite started a mobile cafe by bringing a tablecloth, cups, tea and coffee and encouraging us to bring flasks and enjoy Christine's wonderful home baking. Now everybody brings something - croissants, sausage rolls, cheese, biscuits. We have spare cups and passers-by are welcome to join us.

In the meantime, we are a recognised body in the town. We had a talk from the RNLI. We have fundraisers, a pink swim for cancer support, a swim for Parkinson awareness and not to forget the social get-togethers. Walkers and runners tell us how uplifting it is to see us. Who knows - maybe all of this will lead to more development of our beach facilities. Two of our members invested in a mobile sauna. What a pleasure for the eye the colourful huts at Redbarn are! What a luxury a shower would be or at least a water tap to wash the sand off our feet and gear.

We are here to stay and grow - Youghal Sea Swimmers - a magical group.

Helen Keane

I love to be beside the sea,
It's part of me.
There's no fear or worries,
When you're in the sea.
It's just me and the sea.

Marguerite Hurton

MY LOVE OF THE WATER

Recently I have somewhat accidently started helping others to improve their open water swimming through breath work. So I now find myself regularly working in an environment that I love and sharing my love of the water. It was through this forum I was requested to write a little article on that passion and where it came from. I guess I inherited that love from my father who from as early as I can remember had me fishing or swimming in the River Bride. Growing up in a little place called Curraglass, I never remember being interested in geography but was fascinated by the fact that the local stream (Curraglass river) flowed into the River Bride just a few fields from my house. The Bride in turn flowed into the Blackwater at nearby Camphire Bridge about 10km away. Finally, the Blackwater met the sea in Youghal.

My early memories of learning to swim were mainly watching my father cutting reeds on the riverbank to carefully make a sort of buoyancy aid which he put under my chin. On warm sunny Sundays we would go to Youghal, spend the day in and out of the water. Afterwards, we would buy boiling water at one of the houses on the Front Strand to make tea with the sandwiches, followed on rare occasions by a trip to Perks. When I began to work in the family seafood business, I drove to many piers around the coast always with towel and togs behind the seat looking for an opportunity to swim, maybe while waiting for a boat to land or simply inventing an excuse. It was a pleasure to make my living and see the beautiful products landed by the many small fishing boats at the time.

Later in life I took up scuba diving which included search and recovery which reinforced what my father always preached which was to respect the water. The pleasurable side of scuba was another world, watching marine life on its own terms. Ironically up to the time I was diagnosed with prostate cancer in 2017 I had always swam with my head above water with no desire to do otherwise. However, at this stage I decided to learn how to do it and this led to me taking up triathlons and opening another chapter in my love of the water. While I enjoy all parts of triathlon, it is the swim that holds me. When training for Ironman 2022 I would try to do an Ironman a week but found myself cycling maybe 180km, running 45-50 but swimming 12-14km which would be 3 Ironman distances.

Now having sold our family seafood business I find that my changed life has suddenly catapulted me back into the sea. I haven't mentioned all the feel good and health benefits associated with being in the water, but I hope my love for the water is fully recognisable in my words.

Billy C

TO DATE OUR COMMUNITY OF SEA SWIMMERS HAS RAISED OVER

While as a group we are just the average person out to enjoy our daily swim, we have also formed a social aspect to our group. This has enabled us to not only support local charities but also enjoy some festivities of our own.

Christine & Marguerite

CHARITIES SUPPORTED 2020 TO DATE

- Cork Simon Community Charity Swim took place on 20/11/21 and raised €2,290.
- Shine for Shay Swim took place on 22/1/22 and raised €1,986.
- Daffodil Day Swims took place on 20/3/22 & 18/3/23 and raised €4,335.
- RNLI Swim took place on 12/6/22 and raised €725.15
- Fundraiser for Special Olympics
- Sunrise swim in aid of Darkness into Light in May 22 & 23. Swimmers' donation online
- Swim in Pink aid of Breast Cancer Awareness. Swimmers' donation online. 30/10/22
- WorldGODay Swim took place on 20/09/22. Awareness Day.
- We have also supported and swam with Paddy Conaghan's 'Ducking and Driving' a fundraiser for a mental health charity called Gemma's Legacy of Hope
- We have supported the Christmas Swim in aid of St. Vincent De Paul

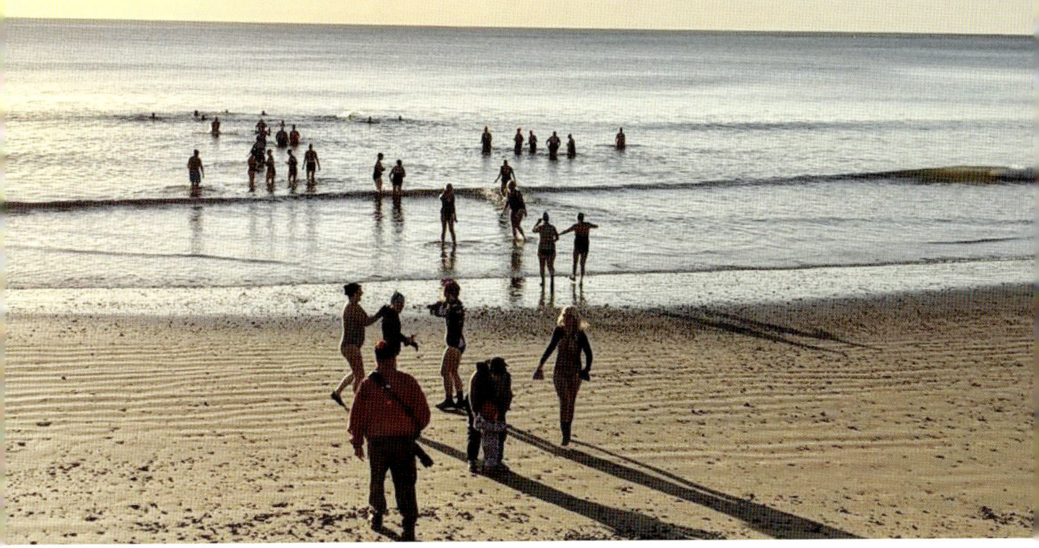

Cork Simon Community Charity Swim

20th November 2021

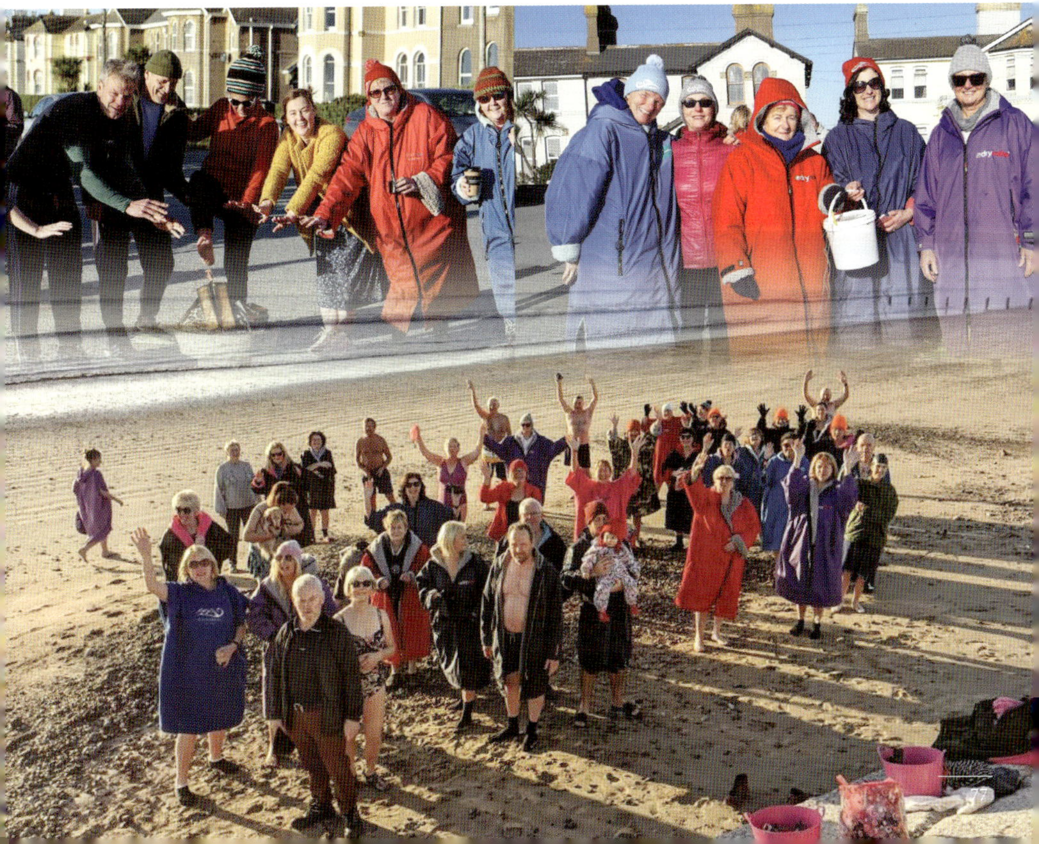

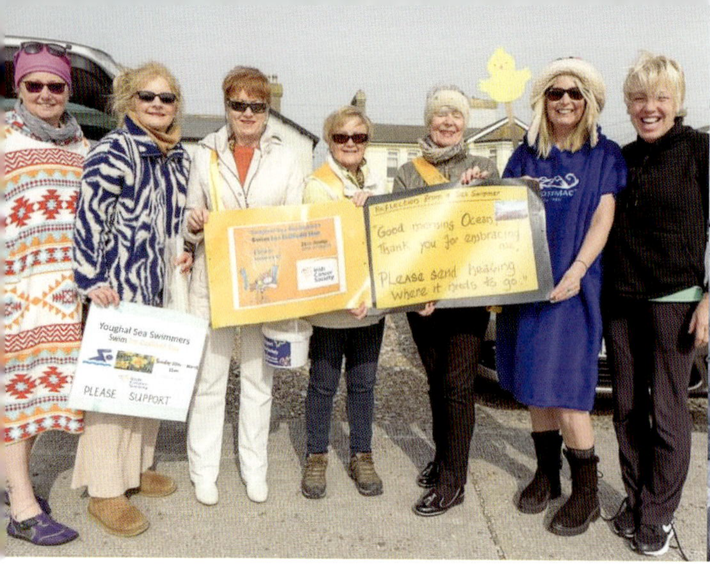

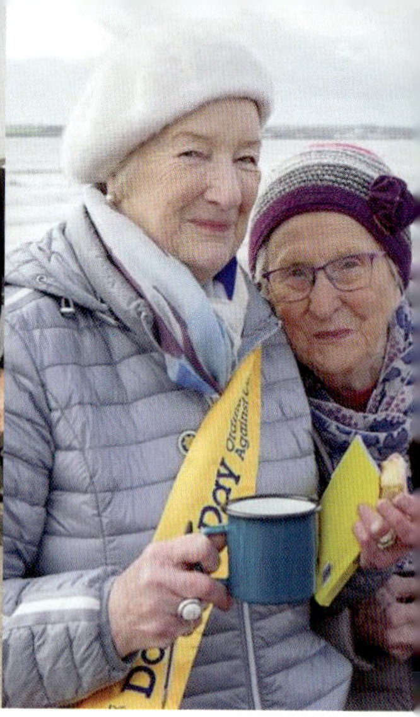

Daffodil Day Swims
20th March 2022 & 18th March 2023

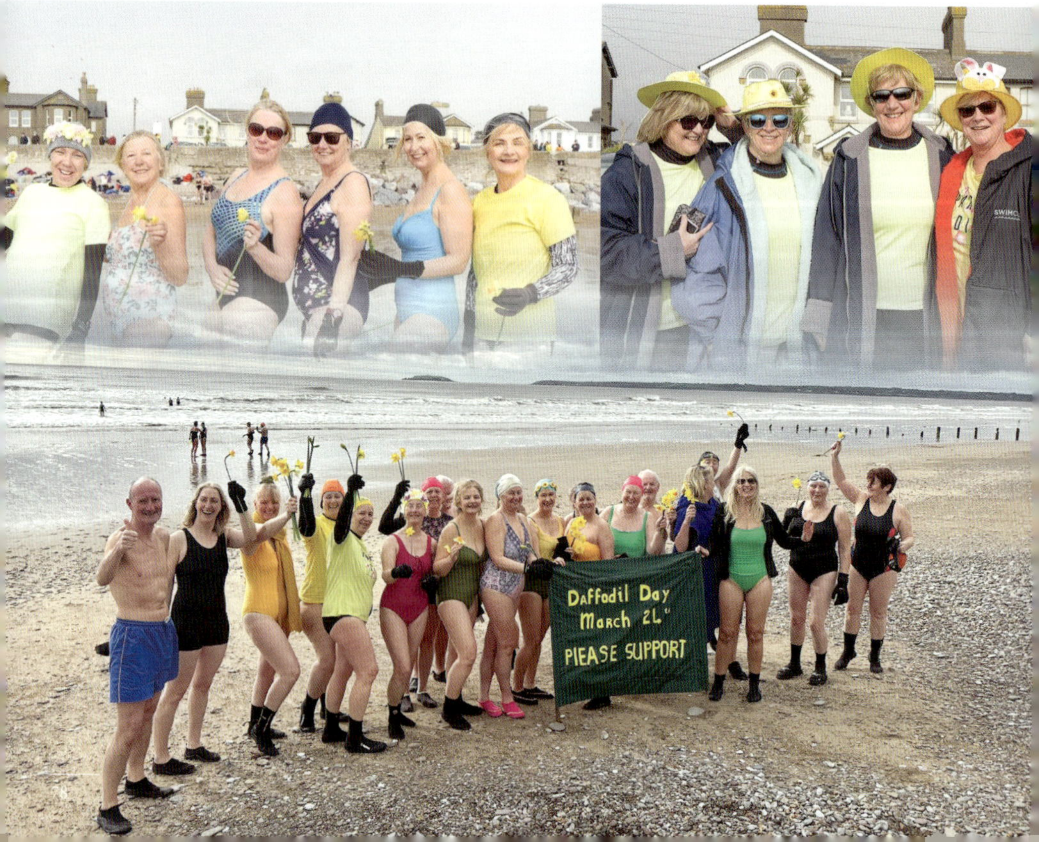

Fund Raising Swims In Aid If National Daffodil Day

'All work and no play makes Jack a dull boy,' this can also be applied to Jill but it most certainly doesn't apply to Youghal Sea Swimmers. This great group started at the beginning of COVID and has made such a difference to the lives of many people and they don't shy away from telling you!

I am not a swimmer but I am a supporter and admirer. As an outsider, I can see the great friendships that have been cemented through swimming. It's great to see them, in groups, bobbing around Youghal beach at different times of the day whatever the weather. The swim is finished with a welcome cuppa and goodies.

I am a volunteer with the Irish Cancer Society. Last year, I asked Linda if maybe the swimmers would do a fundraising swim around National Daffodil Day to raise some much-needed funds. This wonderful group not only swam but also held a raffle. The swimmers donated enough goodies to fill three hampers and twenty four prizes. The swimmers have raised over €4,000 over the last two years. This sum was way beyond anyone's expectations. Such a fantastic morning's work. Since then, they have gone on to have many more fundraising swims, all achieving great success.

Wishing this vibrant group continued success.
Best wishes,

Eileen Donoghue

Shine for Shay Swim
22nd January 2022

SHINE4SHAY

In early January 2022, having been given the rare diagnosis of the genetic disease XLP, the family and friends of 7-year-old local boy Shay McInerny, quickly formed a fundraising committee, to raise as much money as we could to relieve the financial worries for his parents, Deborah and Steve, as the diagnosis meant a move to the UK for a chemotherapy and a stem cell transplant. A Go Fund Me campaign was set up and the call went out to the local community for help.

The very first offer of help came from the local sea swimmer's club. They had a fundraising swim organised in a few short days and their help, support and enthusiasm will never be forgotten. This selfless tribe of swimmers organised prizes, sold tickets, provided hot drinks and treats for the seasoned professionals and the not so seasoned amateur swimmers on the day. It was a sight to behold seeing a community come together on that fresh January morning, where the local radio station broadcast the event across the airways and the Cork Hill Pipe Band members celebrated these amazing supporters in music.

The local emergency services and Gardaí were on hand to offer support if needed and buckets were shaken and money poured in. While we all watched in awe as the swimmers, young and old, took to the open sea, Deborah, Steve and Shay watched via video call from Temple Street Hospital with pride and admiration , as their friends, families and complete strangers took to the water in support of this little boy who stole our hearts.

Just shy of €2100 was raised on that most memorable of January mornings. Shay's treatment is still ongoing and will be for many months to come. But the kindness and thoughtfulness of the Youghal Sea Swimmers who came on board without hesitation, will not be forgotten. That morning proved to us all that when one of our tribe is in need, the rest of the tribe will be there to help in whatever way they can. These sea swimmers truly are some of the best in our community. Míle Buíochas from the proud members of the Shine4Shay committee and from the McInerney family.

Valerie McCarthy

RNLI Swim
12th June 2022

WORLD GO DAY

World Go Day (Gynaecological Oncology) this year focused on Uterine Cancer. This year's campaign emphasised the importance of keeping active. Supporters were encouraged to participate in a Dip or Dance campaign. But we sea swimmers dipped AND danced. We dipped and then enjoyed a high calorific breakfast of sausage rolls, smashed avocado, croissant and scones with jam and cream and cupcakes. And then we danced. We had great fun and a very enjoyable morning.

Any sea swimmer who promised to swim on September 20th got a purple GO swim hat. We all entered the tide together with unmistakable purple hats and the photos of this event were posted on social media.

Research carried out on behalf of INGO found that 60% of Irish women were unaware of the signs and symptoms of Uterine Cancer.

This year's sea swim was an awareness campaign and not a fundraiser.

Swim in Pink aid of Breast Cancer Awareness
30th October 2022

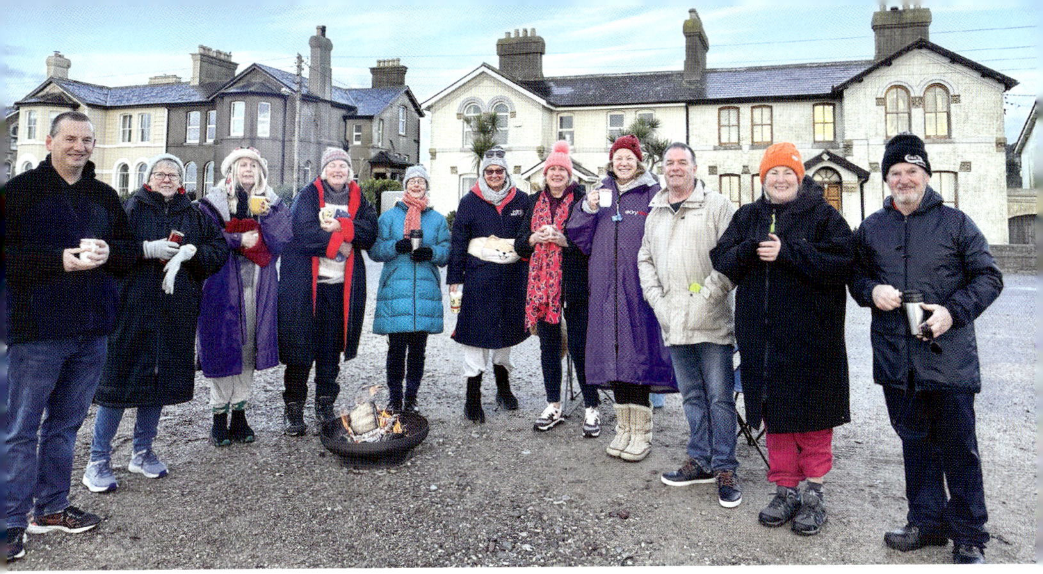

Fundraiser for Down Syndrome Cork
17 December 2022

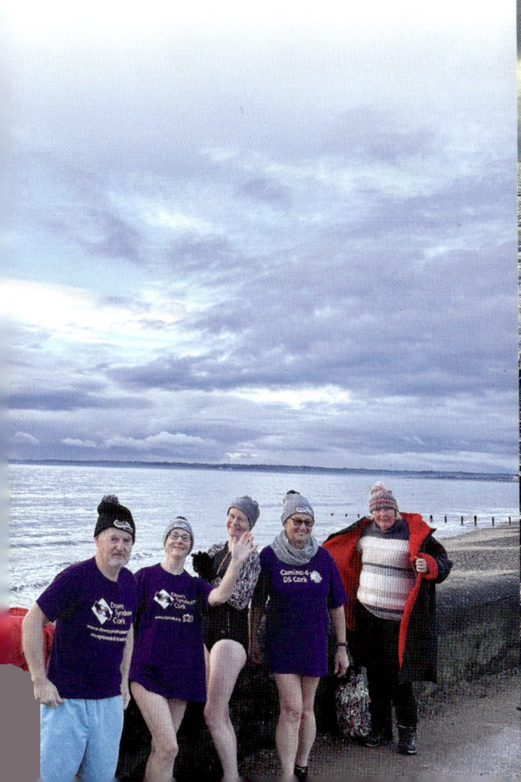

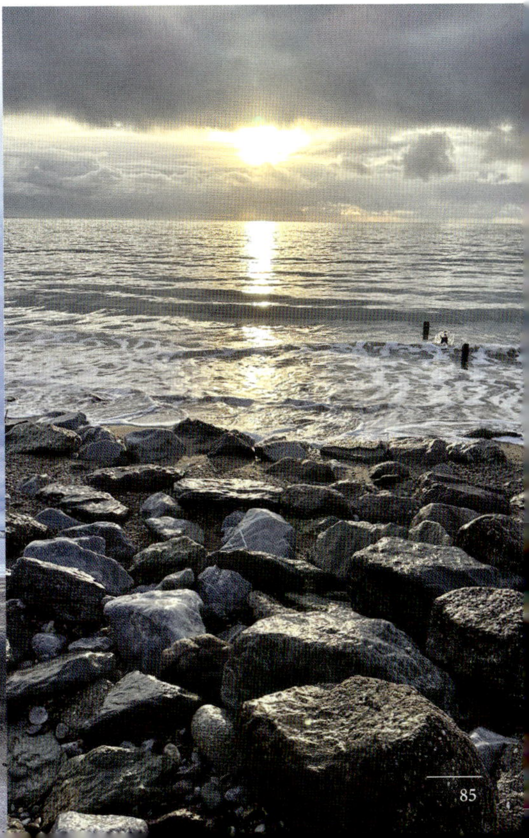

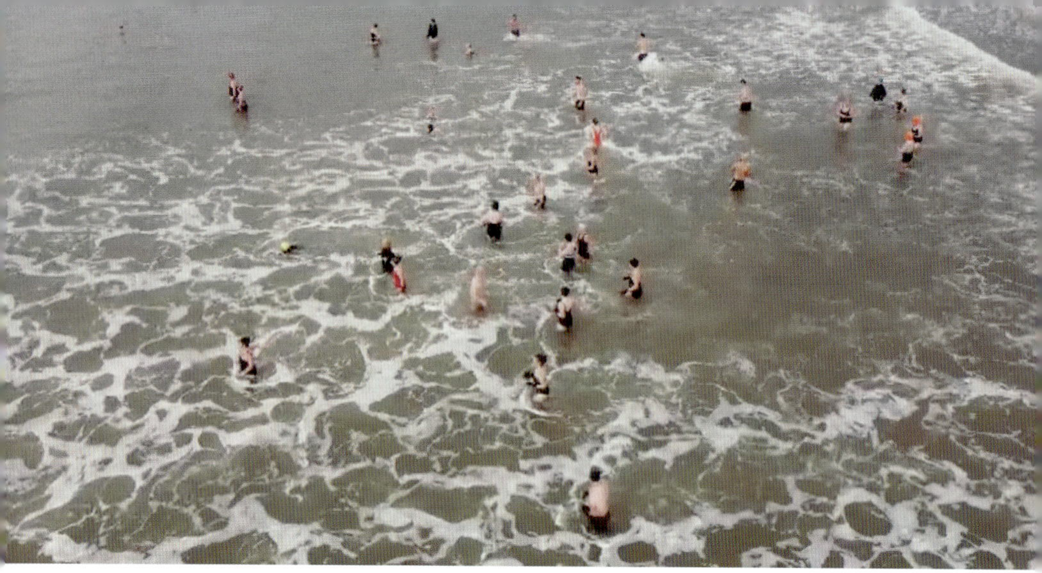

Swim with Paddy Conaghan's 'Ducking and Driving'
11th January 2022

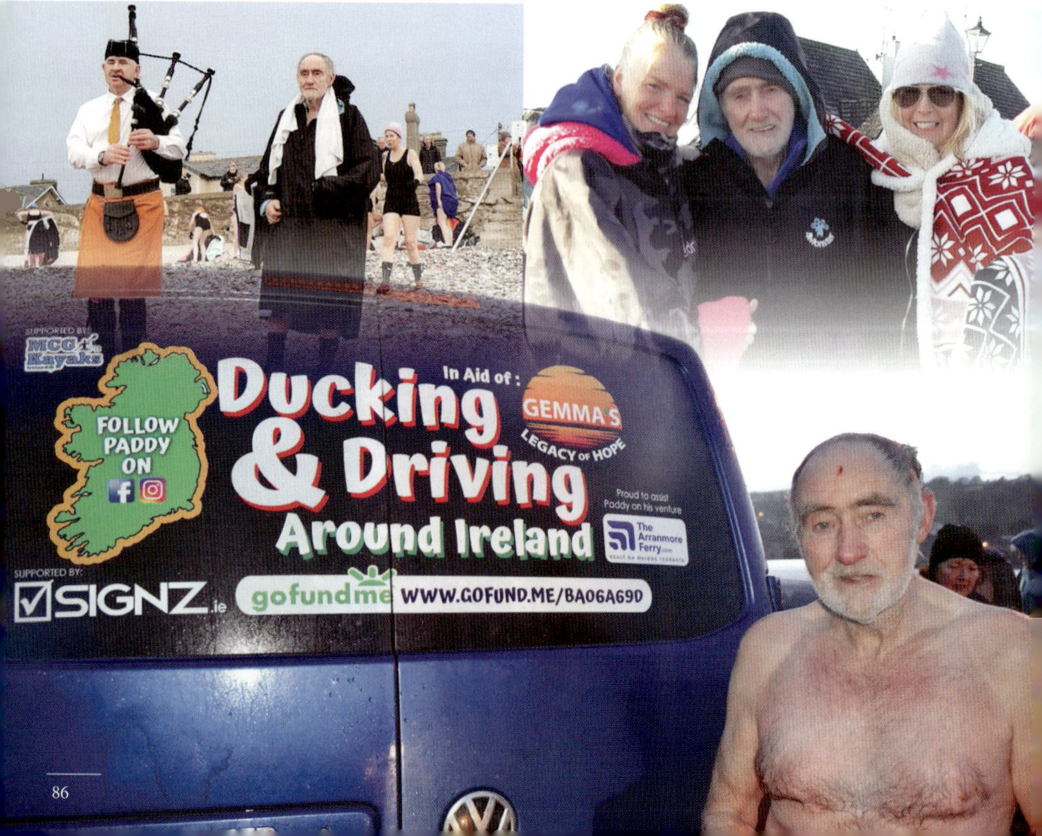

Swim in aid of Darkness into Light
May 2022 & 2023

SPECIAL OLYMPICS

The first fundraiser organised by Youghal Sea Swimmers was in support of "Freezin' for a Reason" in aid of the Special Olympics. This was inspired by the powerful difference being involved in the Special Olympics has made in the life of Sean Coleman and all the other athletes who participate throughout the year in various sports clubs throughout Ireland, supported by volunteers.

The fundraiser took place on 20th December, 2020. It was a beautiful sunny Sunday morning, the tide was full and happening as it did in the midst of COVID, all participants were delighted to have socially distanced fun in the sea in aid of a wonderful cause. The event raised €1,010 for the charity.

OUR OLYMPIAN!

My name is Sean Coleman. My love of the sea started in Redbarn when I was a toddler paddling there. My ambition was to get over to the island. I made a few attempts to get there and on one occasion my mother had to get an off-duty army officer to swim out and bring me back when I was heading across on my bodyboard.

I joined swimming classes organised by the Cork Down's Syndrome Association in Lota when I was 3 years old to help with the development of my motor skills. I had to take a break for a year as I had open heart surgery in Crumlin Children's Hospital when I was 4. I then joined the Cork Special Olympics Swimming Club, Mayfield and have been training with and competing for the club since. I won gold, silver and bronze at the Ireland Games in 2014 which qualified me for selection for the Irish team in the Special Olympics World Games in Los Angeles in 2015.

Participating in the games was a great experience. I got fantastic support from family, friends, my employers SuperValu and the whole community. My swimming coach, Chris O'Halloran, came to Aura in Youghal to coach me in the lead up to the games. I won two silver medals in the 25m front crawl and backstroke and was proud to bring my medals home to Youghal.
I still love to swim in Redbarn and Youghal Front Strand in the summer and I haven't given up on my ambition to swim across to Capel Island.

Sean Coleman

YOUGHAL FRONT STRAND
⭐Day 16⭐ Part 1
Dip a Day for @jackandjillcf
We met a really lovely group of swimmers from @youghalseaswimmers2020
We were invited to join them for their post swim brekkie @priorycoffeeco and our best boy 🐶 @tedwiththebighead2 was allowed join us ❤️

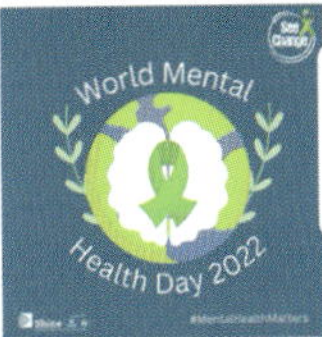

Green Ribbon
12 October 2022

THE SEA IS A GREAT LEVELLER

One of my most abiding memories from my childhood was the excitement of a trip to the seaside. The pinnacle of such trips was the joy of running with total abandonment into the sea, for me there was no fear or trepidation, just the delight to frolic in the waves and feel the power and comfort of the sea's warm embrace. Over the years as I moved on with my life. I consigned such wonderful moments to the memory box entitled 'Childhood Memories', only to be opened when I sought refuge from the demands of a working life, family life and all the routines that I had built to help me become a well organised parent. Not knowing then as I realise now - that routines can sometimes entrap rather than free the spirit.

However, despite parking the positive memories of my sea adventures I always ensured that my children were introduced to all the wonders that the sea could offer, in particular that they too had the opportunity to experience the same joy and abandonment. While I encouraged them to immerse themselves in the sea, I noticed that I had developed a block or fear for sharing their passion for the water... it was too cold, too rough or even too salty! As my children, now young adults began to find their own paths in life, they kept alive their love of the sea and in particular for sea swimming and I often wondered why I hadn't taken advantage of the same opportunity. This idea of a lost opportunity got me thinking and in recent times on my daily walks along the Front Strand in Youghal, I would observe a group of women and men, in all weathers, stride bravely into the sea with the joy and abandonment that I had once experienced as a child. I would stop and watch them in complete awe and admiration.

I soon realised that the sea had not changed but I had and sought to find the key to unlocking my childhood memory box for good. It soon became apparent to me that I was gripped by fear, the fear of getting into the cold sea. I knew I had to conquer this fear and just let go and go for it (easier said then done). I longed to overcome this fear and share in the fun that this amazing group of sea swimmers were experiencing. By chance, I was offered the opportunity to join the group via a WhatsApp link and this was the start of my return to what I thought was just a swim in the sea.

The morning the WhatsApp message went out for a swim at 9am, was without exaggeration, one of those life changing moments for me. I had to conquer my inner fear and just go for it and immerse myself in the sea. As I made my way down to the beach every reason why I shouldn't go through with this made themselves clear – "This was just a childhood thing, grow up and act your age, what are you trying to prove? You're the one that puts the heating on in the car at every opportunity, almost sits on the radiator in winter... what are you at??! Now, just turn around and go home and you can say that you tried".

As I struggled with my inner thoughts, my feet were travelling in the direction of the sea and before I knew it, I was in the midst of a sea swimming group... 'Oh God! I can't turn back now. What will I do!' With the shock of the cold water imminent, my heart was thumping and multiple emotions were swirling around my head. But the group were always there encouraging me in a calm way to take the plunge. Someone calmly spoke and said "After three we will just get down". One, two, three! I was immersed. I felt a huge adrenaline rush, an almost out of body experience. In an instant, I had suddenly conquered my fear and reconnected with my carefree spirit. All my negative thoughts as to why I should not partake in such a cathartic and revitalising experience were literally washed away. Members of the group encouraged and supported me to keep the activity going and I have.

The 9am morning swims are now part of my daily routine, a good routine that gives me the space to reconnect with the sea, embrace my inner self but more importantly to partake in a community of like-minded people that are called the Youghal Community of Sea Swimmers. The camaraderie of this group is so beautiful and simple, we all enjoy the sea as it is a great leveller. In the sea there are no barriers, we are all one, we are simply peeled back to our basic selves, take us, or leave us for what we are. And what are we? Simply a community that has conquered our fear of swimming in the sea, enjoying the feeling of peace washed over us as we are surrounded by the vastness of the sea. For me, every day the swim challenges me to concentrate on my surroundings, it has reawakened my inner child to experience the joy of the sea, to let the worries of life float away from me during this special time. In short, to live in the here and now with a sea swimming family and feel blessed that I have fully found my tribe.

Fiona Horgan

Sea Swimming is Memory

A good place to start is my father taking me to learn about sea swimming in Coolmain, a sheltered inlet near Kilbrittain. Here the waves lapped gently and there was no great drag in the tide, it was a great place to learn. He had a ritual which involved running into the water, diving in to become fully climatised and then running back out. He said the first time was for the water and the second time was for the swim!

I followed suit and shivering in my coldness, he gave me my learning instructions. At my shoulder level he held his arms out like a fork-lift and cradled me while I flapped and flayed. Eventually, maybe part instinct, I slithered off like a fish into the water and after a few scrambled strokes I went downwards and had that first memorable, beautiful taste of seawater!

After a few trips to Coolmain I got the rhythm and stretched my strokes to almost match his, but I think he slowed his to match mine! Eventually, we graduated to the wide beach in Garrettstown, where all the family and friends gathered on summer Sundays. Here there was generally a strong swell and good surfing waves, so you had to stay on your toes, literally! It was always a group swim and the golden rule was that nobody entered the water alone and nobody stayed in the water alone.

My father and his group had a tradition when leaving the water: turning back to the sea at waist level they splayed their arms backwards and scooped the water out at the coming waves. It was a gesture of acknowledgement, of unity and of thanks. As my ancient aunt said "You always give thanks when you leave the water on two feet." And so, I joined the culture of sea swimmers and in the tradition of my family became a salt swimbee!

While the culture of the sea and the salt smell was always in my thinking, this was challenged when I moved to Geneva. I ended up swimming in Lac Leman under the famous sprout – in flat, dark, un tidal, tasteless, glacial cold water. It was swimming, but not as I knew it and I never lived inland again.

With my own family we lived near the beach in Malahide and swam at High Rock and Low Rock. It was the calm Irish Sea, but I carried on the history and initiated all my kids into sea swimming, adding a few new strokes to lengthen the tradition! Now we are back in Youghal and sucking Atlantic salt again as well as swimming!

The history of all my family is tucked away in the sea memory library and each time I go in the water now, I dive deep to trove the treasure.
Sea swimming is memory.

Frank Down

A LINE IN THE SAND

At the end of April 2020, I drew a line in the sand and decided to take early retirement. After thirty years dealing with the public, it was time to begin a new phase of my life. The making of the decision was daunting but once I announced my intentions, my mind was at ease. The biggest fear I had was anticipating that I would miss the interaction with people as this interaction was central to my working life. My decision to take early retirement coincided with the initial restrictions resulting from COVID which was going to make my new life even more restrictive.

Little did I know that starting sea swimming (dipping rather!) from May 1st, 2020, was going to take care of all those fears. Initially, the group of swimmers were few, but once people could see and feel the benefits of sea swimming the numbers grew rapidly. My daily interaction now revolves around sea temperatures, seaweed, tidal times, jellyfish and dry robes. Strangers have become friends, united in the joy of sea swimming. The mix of the sea swimming group is truly eclectic, from age to personalities to diving techniques. A day without a swim (dip!) is a day lost. The exhilaration of the water and the buzz of the initial "getting down" is unrivalled. Also, it has made me become the perfect liar in saying, "the water is not too bad today." No, it's baltic!

J.B.S.T.

Sea Swimming & Me

All my life I have lived by the sea,
Every day is different, with a view for me.
As a child we would go to the beach in summer,
We swam every day with my father and mother.
When the summer months ended the swimming was done,
An end to the joy, the laughter and the fun.

I walked the beach nearly every day of my life,
I watched swimmers dip in winter and wondered what it would be like.
I was always tempted to just take the dip,
But not on my own, so I gave it a skip.
I spoke with the swimmers who swam all year around,
The stories they told me of the happiness they found.

So, one day in winter maybe three years ago,
My friends said to join them and I couldn't say no.
On a cold winter morning I joined the crew,
What a shock to the system, I can tell you, I was blue!!
But after my swim, the feeling was so good,
I continued to dip, every day that I could!

Our group started small, with just maybe a few,
But each day that we swam, there was always someone new.
The friends I have met, which is down to our swim,
It would encourage anyone, just to dip and get in.
So the 9 o'clock slot in Claycastle is the place to be!

Cars and bikes abandoned for the run into the sea,
Dry robes in all colours line the wall,
Buckets and bins, some big and small.
After the swim, the table is set up,
For everyone to join together for a quick 'cup.'

So thank you for the friends I have made in the sea,
For the laugh and the joy, it has brought me.
For the feel-good factor that we all get,
And thank you for the sea. It is how we all met.

Ella O'Siochrú

THE RIGHT PLACE AT THE RIGHT TIME

One of the lovely things in life is the ability to swim. Consequently, being in the right place at the right time is also a very interesting thing, when one can swim.

The story I am about to tell you really starts in 1952, when, as a young man, a young boy in fact, I learned to swim in a little town called Courtown Harbour. The thing about it is, I went swimming with my father, thinking I knew how to swim and jumped into the canal. Luckily enough my father was there to pull me out. He then brought me around the back, onto the beach and taught me how to swim in a matter of minutes! The reason why I am recalling this story is because of the fact that the story I'm about to tell you is also about being in the right place at the right time.

Around 1958 I was going to a boarding school in Midleton College. At the time we used to live in T.P. Walsh's, which was the hardware shop in the middle of Youghal town, with the back facing out onto the quays. If people cast their minds back, they will remember one of the ships from the making of Moby Dick was lying there in the water and unfortunately it had deteriorated over the years. When I was in Midleton we used to get one day off a month, when we could come home to our parents. Now my parents had left the house, my father had sold it, but I still had the key to the front door. I actually loved living in T.P. Walsh's and I had an opportunity to go in and hang around the shop for a few hours before it was handed over to the new owners.

While I was killing the day, I was at the back gate and I happened to see a young chap jump onto the old ship. I was talking to our good friend and neighbour next-door, Mrs Buttimer, you'll all remember Nora. After a few seconds I excused myself from Nora. As I was moving away, I noticed the young boy had disappeared. So consequently, I toddled on over and looked down into the bottom of the boat. I then realised that the young boy was floundering around in the water, which you really couldn't call water. It was a mixture of muck, diesel and general rubbish that had accumulated over the years. I realised that if I didn't go down and pull the young chap out, we were going to have a tragedy on our hands.

Unfortunately, I couldn't jump in because of the fact that there was a large beam running along the bottom of the ship. You couldn't see this because of the amount of water. So, I had to scamper down. Eventually I got down, waded in and swam across to the young fella. I caught him by the scruff of the neck and pulled him out. I got him up onto the beam which was running along the middle of the ship. I then realised that there was no way I could get him up onto the deck. Luckily enough I had learned the 'Fireman's Lift' in Midleton College. So consequently, I got him up onto my shoulders and then up the very steep steps. I had only just reached the top of the steps when, lo and behold, I realised I just couldn't go any further. So, I tossed him over onto his tummy. With that he hit the timber and a huge gush of water came out of his mouth. I then clambered up onto the deck and hauled him up. I laid him on the deck and after a couple of seconds or minutes, I can't remember exactly now as it was a long time ago, he coughed and spluttered. He looked at me as if to say... who, what... you know he made no sense. Anyhow he scampered off home and that was the end of that. I didn't see him anymore. I went back inside, into T.P. Walsh's, threw all my clothes and everything else into the washing machine. I did a clean up job on myself, aired my clothes on the old airer and moseyed on back to Midleton College. And that was the end of that because as I already said we were moving out. We had sold the business and were going to live in Dublin.

So, years had passed and I never heard another word about it. However, a few years back I was sitting in a bar beside my late friend Paddy Neville and his wife Betty Neville, she was one of the Watkins and we were talking away. I looked up and under the mural in the bar – the lounge now – I said to Paddy and Betty 'See that boat there. I remember as a young fella pulling a boy out of that'. And with that there was total silence in the bar and I kind of said 'Oh Jesus, don't tell me now something serious happened... did he die or what?' So, I told them the story about it and they both started to laugh. And by the way, there was more of Betty's family there and they couldn't believe what I was telling them. So anyhow no more about that.

The following day I was coming down the road and I met Mrs Watkins and she said 'So t'was you who saved the little devil!'

Well anyhow, back to my story. So, I told them what had happened and all the rest and then I discovered that it was actually Betty Watkin's brother who I had pulled out, Timmy, who died a few years ago. I'm sure I've left bits and pieces of the story out but as you can understand you're going back to 1958/59, quite a few years ago.

The thing I'm trying to say, as I said in the preamble of this is... It's an amazing thing to be in the right place at the right time, to do the right thing.

Norman McDonald

(Transcribed from a voice recording)

SUMMER MEMORIES AT THE FRONT STRAND

In the summer, the children from Sarsfield Terrace relocated to the Front Strand. We were southerners, unlike the northerners from the other end of town who swam in the pool at the Slob Bank. We followed the sun and migrated south to paradise. Armed with just towels and togs, we embarked on a familiar route down the Golf Links Road, past Bobby Atkins' corner, guided by the catchy tunes of The Archies' "Sugar Sugar" emanating from Perks Funfair. As we descended the steps beside the Atlantic and Pacific hotel, the aroma of cooked food wafted from the back of the building. After crossing the road through the strand gap, we reached our oasis. School was out for summer. Heaven!

You didn't know if it was high tide or low tide, it didn't matter. It looked like a mile away when the tide was out. We'd hastily change into our togs and an older member of the group would race towards the water, shouting, "Last one in is a fool!" It was like the charge of the light brigade down the full length of the beach as everyone ran like Ronnie Delaney towards the tide. Try doing that wearing those cheap plastic sandals biting into your heels with the straps missing. Hell!

Bless yourself three times with the sea water as you entered, a short prayer to protect you. "Hail Mary full of... and a crashing wave in the head. You were in and under. This is where you learnt to swim. There were no swimming lessons. You just did the dogs paddle as best you could until eventually you could outstretch your arms and swim like the others.

The second breaker as we called it was where everyone congregated. This was our spot. In the sixties the old sea wall was curved and you would slide down into the water's edge at high tide. Here you would dry yourself on the hot concrete and bate the living daylights out of your togs to wring out the water. No one knew or cared about UV rays or heard of factor 50. When you did get sunburnt your mother would spread white calamine lotion on your back and arms to cool the burning blisters. Torture.

Later in the early seventies the new promenade was built. An expansive giant flat concrete surface overlooking what we thought was the finest beach in Ireland. As teenagers you mixed with different people. Swimming off the promenade was the greatest of fun. Swimming from breaker to breaker and diving off the top of the wooden groynes. At high tide we'd impress onlookers with handstands and legs protruding from the water. Then disappear under the water and swim as far away as possible, leaving the curious "Corkies" on the promenade bewildered.

In 1975, the blockbuster movie Jaws was in the cinema. The late Joe Horgan was a great swimmer and he could swim breaker to breaker. Joe would pretend he was being attacked by a shark splashing about and waving his hands in the water then being dragged under. Shouts of "Shark" from the group. Somehow he would mimic being pulled along the top of the water like in the film. You can only imagine the Corkies' faces in complete horror as they watched from the promenade. It was only a teenage prank but a bit reckless. Another time we would try to swim like Patrick Duffy in the American TV series "Man from Atlantis' with your legs joined together moving up and down like Flipper the dolphin. It took a while but eventually we kinda mastered the style. It worked - until several dislocated vertebrae later and a visit to the chiropractor, we soon went back to the breaststroke.

Not satisfied enough to be playing air guitar imitating the songs of the time, at one stage we formed an underwater rock band. Underwater the drummer banged away like Stuart Copeland from The Police. I hit the chords like a rock star but instead of air guitar, this time it was water guitar. We found it hard to find someone to do lead vocals!

The promenade was a great place to walk, especially to be seen promenading along the strip with your finest clothes or beach wear. For us boys it was denim, in fact double denim, flares, bell bottoms and multi coloured tank tops and cheesecloth shirts. The girls mini skirts, bell-bottoms, hippie look. Flowing maxi dresses and platform shoes. At the start of the promenade the boys sat on the high wall across from Perks. This high wall served as a gathering place for the boys to watch girls go by, much like a modern-day dating app. One day, the lads were admiring the scenery and along came this beach beauty wearing a red Baywatch bikini. Like a row of dominoes falling, with elbows in the ribs that left you breathless, one of the group excitedly yelled "Lads, quick, take a look at that!". All heads turned left. As the blonde walked toward the group, one voice deflated their excitement, "Forget it lads, she's local!" She wasn't exotic enough for the Youghal boy teenagers!

That night when you got home after another long three-parter day, morning sports on the road in the terrace, soccer, rounders, afternoon swim on the beach and nighttime gallivanting before you'd eventually get home to watch a bit of tele. The weather forecaster on RTE, "Tomorrow will be fine and sunny" pointing at the isobars lines on the map of Ireland. This was always followed by my father saying "Don't believe a word from him. He never gave a good weather forecast in his life". He was right. No swimming tomorrow.

Michael Hussey

Reasons for Swimming

Everybody swims for different reasons. For me it was medicine for mind and body.

I joined the community of sea swimmers in the autumn of 2020.The group was much smaller but has grown exponentially since. It is a very close-knit community and that is mainly what has attracted me to it. The community of sea swimmers extends a warm welcome to all comers and the camaraderie is wonderful.

The call to arms arrives via Whats App each morning around 7.30 am and the thumbs up follows. This is an incentive to get out of bed, get the gear ready and head for the beach.

Sea swimming/dipping helps release stress and relax the muscles. With a hot cuppa and Mrs. Berry's cupcakes and a chat, it is a wonderful start to the day.

The first year the weather was colder so we jumped in the car and headed straight for home to dress and warm up. Last year, the weather was milder and we managed to dress on the beach after our swim and then enjoy the cuppa and goodies.
Sea swimming became very popular and people swam at different times and in different groups, which suited their circumstances.

The 9am time suited me and the shrieks as we hit the cold water could be heard in the town. On Sunday mornings we had breakfast in The Priory, Brunch Box or in the Boardwalk on the Mall after the swim.

We did sunrise and sunset swims, Pink swims and Go swims, Christmas and Solstice swims and candlelit swims. The social aspect of the group is also important and social outings and raffles are held on a regular basis.

Safety is a priority and everybody looks out for each other. Advice and tide times are posted on the sea swimmer's Whats App when appropriate.

Anonymous

SWIMMING FOR UKRAINE

FLOATING

The feeling of freedom
A deafening silence
Floating through waves
The world in balance.

Vast space surrounds
Empty myself to the sun
Beneath the dark waves
The world is one.

Body at ease
A mind at peace
Weightless in water
All worries cease.

Time loses meaning
The sea holds me
Here in the waves
I am finally free.

Aisling Curran

MY MEDITATION

It is a great fortune that from the windows of my house I can admire the sea... in assorted colours and moods.

Since I lived in Youghal, going to the beach became a daily event and I would sometimes see and praise people washed by the waves, regardless of the season. It was a rare sign, however, at the beginning of my life in Youghal, six years ago.

My swimming in Youghal started with Polish friends who swam in one of the winters and led me by the hands into the chilly water. It was icy and not very pleasant and yet somehow it pulled me in with great force. My friends stopped swimming after the winter, or they did it very rarely but I liked it and came increasingly often. I found how beneficial it was for my feelings.

After some time, while walking or swimming, I started seeing a group of people who were extremely happy to enter the water together, so I also started to come to this place, instead of going somewhere alone. Somehow, I naturally joined the group, whose path is incredibly friendly.

When I go into the water, I feel such a spiritual connection. I feel like I have crossed some invisible lines. I lift my head towards the sun and give thanks for everything I have, for my life, for my every day, for my family, for my friends and I whisper back my prayer in thanks for everything.

This is my meditation, an inert encounter with God, in my understanding of God.

Swimming in the sea gives me incredible power and positivity and always makes my day.

Gosia Pieniazek

MIDLIFE MAGIC

My love affair with the ocean began almost two years ago following a cancer diagnosis. Initially, I felt devastated and the dark night of my soul came, bringing with it immense grief and an infinite well of tears. As well as the emotional pain, there was also the physical pain that prevented me doing what I enjoyed – running, dancing, yoga, gardening – even walking my precious dog, Shelby.

As I re-emerged from the dark days, I began to think there must be something that I can do, that I can both enjoy and challenge myself with. Sea swimming kept popping up and I resisted for a while because I was someone who did not like the cold one bit! One day in June I got a notion, rummaged for a pair of togs and said to my cousin Marie who is a seasoned sea swimmer herself, " I'm joining you today." And I have not stopped! Sea swimming has been an unexpected gift in the midst of the storm and I feel so incredibly grateful every day to have discovered the magic of the ocean.

I have quite literally fallen in love with the ocean – she is my soul medicine. My daily dip fills me with joy and lifts me up in every way imaginable , physically, emotionally and spiritually. No matter how I am feeling on a given day, I can sink myself into her soothing healing embrace, connect with my own presence and rejoice in nature and the beauty that is all around me. It is a magical unique experience everyday and it sets me up for the day ahead. It is also the place where I have the privilege of meeting with the wonderful sea swimming community of Youghal, the group that grows and grows. Thank you to Linda, for starting this amazing group. Each of us is drawn to the ocean for our own reasons, a place where we can just be in the present moment where all is well. I love that friends and family have also taken up sea swimming and it is now a joyful experience for them too. We chat, we laugh, we scream, some of us more than others – moi being one! I do enjoy screaming and laughing as I dance on the waves. It is a wonderful release. I am breathing in new life and joy into my lungs. I feel like my inner child comes out to play and it is so much fun.

Each day, as I saunter down the beach with my fellow swimmers and wade into the tide with a big smile on my face, I recite my prayer (thank you Marie).
"Good morning Ocean, thank you for embracing me. Please send healing where it needs to go". All is well.

I have dipped through radiotherapy, chemotherapy and everything in between and I know that mother ocean will be there to ease the journey of life, whatever it may bring. In the midst of a storm, there are many blessings to be found when you have the right kind of eyes to see.

Olivia Pyne

dryrobe
dryrobe

RAIN OR SHINE

My name is Eileen. I am 65 years of age. I am a mam of six children, all grown up, ranging in age from 27 to 41 and I now have seven grandchildren, who are all amazing.

I started sea swimming, daily, on the 1st of June 2020, during COVID. I usually go in the morning as I feel it sets me up for the day, with a really 'feel good' and energising spin off. Unless I'm on granny duty and then I go later in the day. I count my strokes and can do up to 400 or maybe 500 each morning. This helps me to change focus from the temperature of the water and brings me into the present.

About 6 months ago I started swimming with a group of ladies. We swim every morning at 8:30 am in Garryvoe. People ask me how the water is? It must be cold. I tell them we are lucky to have a free spa on our doorstep!

I still work two days a week in retail but have my swim before work. I swim no matter what the weather, rain or shine, unless it is too rough or dangerous. I asked one of the ladies I swim with, her name is Fiona, 'What does sea swimming mean to you?' She said 'It sets me up for the day'. We have a Whats App group set up and we keep in touch on this. I would highly recommend sea swimming. It is hard to describe the feeling but I think it is good for the mind, body and soul.

Go for it! Start swimming in the summer when the water is warmer and see how long you can keep going.

Eileen

Being at One with Nature

I took up swimming many years ago, when I was a kid. Rather I was forced to take up swimming!

My encounter with the water happened at the Slob Bank. My older brother asked me if I could swim. I mumbled 'no' to which he replied 'You gotta learn sometime, no time like the present'. Then he pushed me in! Thus beginning my lifelong love affair with the water.

To me swimming is exhilarating, being at one with nature. It's also a great social occasion. It promotes a feeling of wellbeing. There's something about the water that invites all of us swimmers to leap, jump or dive. It releases us from the gravity of earth. It lifts our spirits, minds and bodies.

Noel Cronin CRY.

I LOVE TO GO A WANDERING ALONG THE STRANDS...

On the 10th April I was born at home at 3 Lee Road adjacent to the River Lee. I was the youngest of five. At the age of 3, we moved to the city centre as my grandmother retired and my parents took over the pub "The Tostal Inn", 46 Grattan Street. We had very little green space there but we had a public swimming pool beside the City Hall.

My first experience of learning to swim was when my father brought my sister Sheila and I on his bicycle to Blackrock. He put me on the cross bar and Sheila at the back. A little way beyond the Castle, the water in the estuary on high tide filled up a concrete pool. We were very excited to go there with dad to swim. On the way back my sister's foot got caught in the back wheel so we ended up at the Mercy Hospital, just a street away from our pub.

At the age of 7, I joined the Brigin's. They were part of The Catholic Guides of Ireland. Every year we went to summer camp at Hyde's Farm in Redbarn. We slept in three railway carriages and another for dining. A small makeshift kitchen and an oratory where a priest came to say mass every Sunday. We were in the field at the seafront. We made campfires on the strand and sang together. We hiked many miles on the strand and back the road, collecting flowers for the altar for Sunday mass. We sang:

"I love to go a wandering
Along the strands of Youghal,
And as I go, I love to sing.
We're happy girl guides all."

The trains out of the city to Youghal were full to capacity every summer weekend. My Auntie Peggie (Margaret) had eight children but she always brought three or four of us with her as my mother had to work in the bar. These were great times for us. We always bought the big pot of tea up at Claycastle and we brought lots of bread and jam sandwiches with us. We grew up with a wonderful relationship with all our cousins as my mother and her family were very close. People had very little money in the fifties and sixties. Most of the children went free on the train as the ticket master turned a blind eye. My father rented a car from a friend during the summer for a few days and most times we ended up at Youghal or Robert's Cove. He had five children or more in the back seat. There were no seat belts in the cars then.

At the age of 8 my sister and I joined the Dolphin Swimming Club. We learned to swim really well and competed in the galas held at Eglantine Pool beside the City Hall. After our swim we went home through the city streets. Our first stop was the Cold Storage Co. on the South Mall where we got an enormous ice cream wafer for a couple of pence. We didn't mind at all the sore eyes we had from the chlorine as we licked our ice cream all the way home. We were very happy kids.

In the summer months, the Lee Baths outdoor pool opened for the public. Every weekend we walked up the Mardyke to the Lee Baths and had great fun in the outdoors. We had diving boards at three different levels. A deep pool and a knee-high pool for young children. There was plenty of room for everyone.

My husband Jack and I married in 1971. We moved to the Grove's Bar in Blackpool in 1977 as my mother had passed away. When the children were young, we took them to Mayfield Pool for swimming lessons. We spent our summer holidays in a mobile home in Summerfield at Youghal Beach. These were very happy years with lots of wonderful memories made with my family. Our children were good swimmers. They had the sea at their doorstep. We retired in 1995 from the pub as we had built the Bed & Breakfast next door in 1992. In 2014 we retired from the B & B and bought a home in Youghal. When we first moved to Youghal, I was very lonely and missed the company of all the people coming and going in our house in Cork.

I went down to the beach and swam on my own as often as I could and met lots of other people just like myself. Last year I met two sisters who told me about the Sea Swimmers Group that swim a little bit further up the beach. I took courage and asked if I could join them. They opened their arms wide and welcomed me. I have never met a group of people who are so generous with their time, kindness and spirit. They all laugh a lot and help those who are not able to. They make sure to have fun and join together for a swim at 9am each morning and after the swim they sit and chat with tea/coffee and whatever else is brought along. We meet new people every day and swap books, plants, pickles and lots of ideas. I am not lonely anymore and I have joy in my heart to pass onto everyone else. Thank you so much everyone. You have changed my life.

Eileen Corbett

THE RELUCTANT SWIMMER

Oh Sweet Jesus!

It's the sixth of October and I'm standing at the top of the steps looking at a cold, dark sea having foolishly committed to another morning swim. I am surrounded by a keen and enthusiastic group of people who appear genuinely happy to be here as they look forward to immersing themselves in icy baltic water. I would prefer to be warming my glutes in front of the stove while drinking a hot cup of coffee.

If the magical genie appeared my first wish would be to fast forward time by thirty minutes resulting in my swim being finished, dressed in warm clothing and blood once again starting to circulate through my veins heading home for that coffee. Unfortunately, no sign of that genie.

Reluctantly I count out the steps as I head towards the beach. It's time to discard warm clothing and strip to my swim shorts. All around me there is an energy from the group of swimmers who are looking forward to their swim. Swimmers of all ages don their gloves, boots and hats, but I have no need for those – this is my last swim until next July!

I walk towards the water as the easterly wind does its best to slice me in half but there is no turning back now.

"Let's get this done as soon as possible"

The water laps around my feet and it is bitterly cold. Onwards I go… up to my knees now

"What am I doing here?
This is not enjoyable!
Why are they all so happy?"

The ultimate cold water swimming guru, Wimhoff, has said that the cold water does strange things to the brain. This is true because now weird and obscure thoughts flood my head.

"Will the certificate state, cause of death was heart attack or hypothermia?
Will the two Weetabix I had this morning be my last meal on this earth?
Is my good suit clean!"

I'm jolted back to reality as the water hits my stomach. The ice cold temperature of the water takes my breath away so my entire focus must now be on breathing. One of the regulars appears and asks me if I will keep swimming through the winter. Multi tasking has never been a strength of mine so breathing and speaking will be a bridge too far at this moment. After a monosyllabic reply I decide that the easiest way out of this is to go for it and get down.

I immerse myself in the water and instantly regret it. The Lord's name is called but he's not very helpful this morning. This water is absolutely freezing. I struggle to breathe and once again question what I am doing here?

The regulars within the group insist that once immersed in the water one should stay under the water. This is the cold water swimmer's version of Sophie's choice – stay down and struggle to catch your breath or stay upright and let the easterly breeze cut you in half. Decisions, decisions. I manage to immerse myself a few more times and am feeling the cold penetrate every part of my being. I have enough – it's time to head for refuge.

As I walk through the water it does not feel as cold as when I was getting in. Leaving the water and heading for the wall I find myself thinking that it wasn't too bad this morning. I might go again tomorrow…

Colin Donoghue

I START MY DAY WITH A SEA SWIM

I started sea swimming at 13 years of age. After school I'd drop my bag at home, change into my swim gear and run into the sea. I'm now 45 years old and start my day with a sea swim.

I am grateful that I live by the sea. My feet touching the sand and sea water plug me into nature. In the sea my mind is calm. I stretch out my arms and feel my body relaxing. When I come out of the sea I am energised for the day ahead.

I sea swim all year. It gets me out of my comfort zone bringing out my bravery, strength and satisfies my sense of adventure.

All I need is a hat, swim shorts, a towel and my sense of adventure.

After a swim my mind is kinder and clearer. Swimming in the sea is my happy and safe place.

Philip Coles

Are You a Swimmer?

"Are you a swimmer?" they ask me generally when I bump into friends or acquaintances in town in my dry robe or if they hear me ask a fellow swimmer, "were you in today? how was it?" "You couldn't really call it swimming" I answer with a smile, "I just run in and faff around a bit and get out again, by no stretch of the imagination could you call it swimming".

I don't mention the sense of anticipation as I drive in and park, the sense of awe as I look over the wall, noticing the sea, shimmering, deep blue, aquamarine, sparkling in the rising sun or cloudy like the sky, heavy, light, calm, glassy, turbulent or shades and degrees in between. Getting out of the car and walking to the wall, noticing if there's a breeze, a drift, any other mad souls here in the middle of February or September or November. The magnetic pull, the craving in my body to get into the water.. By now, any worries or concerns that I had have receded to the back of my brain, I'm in the moment, pulling on the swimming hat, booties and gloves and becoming absorbed by the beach and the water. I'm part of the landscape, in my natural habitat, at home, at peace. That sense deepens as I enter the water, waves lap and another and another, welcoming me, enveloping me, consistent, always there. The tide coming in and going out as it has been for centuries. I will come and go, it will be here for me while I'm here and long after I'm gone. It will be here, anchoring, holding.

At sunrise as I sink into the sea I notice that my eyes are at where the shimmering of the sun on the water stops. I'm part of the shimmering, part of the sea, part of the sunrise,in my natural habitat, at home, at peace. These are beautiful mornings, wrapping themselves around me, supporting me as I live and breathe.

In the cold days of winter I marvel at how my body craves the cold. After the first few seconds when every fibre is screaming, a feeling of being at ease and alive in the cold seeps in, sharpening all the senses, breathtaking, in awe at the wonder of it all. They're the calm days. There are others that the sea is forceful and demanding to be respected. On those days I wonder ?Will I get in? Will I be able for it? Will it demand too much of me? I've got to know my limits, my body knows its limits and decides for me. Surrender. Let my body guide me, no, not today. And the in-between days, when the waves are crashing but not strong enough to deter me, the exhilaration of diving into a wave or surfing it onto the beach, the joy, the happiness, the beauty, the shared craziness of it all. We're alive, we're free, we're wild beings, being in the wild.

"Are you a swimmer?" they ask me, if I had a word to describe it I'd use it. Words fail me. "You should try it sometime" I say.

Sally O'Connor

WE ARE UNIQUE

Growing up in our beloved Youghal was a privilege that I took for granted and I really did not appreciate the power that this beautiful town can have on you if you open your eyes.

Until 2020, COVID came and with that came lockdown, isolation from your loved ones. Doing grocery drops to my parent's back door was just too hard. I missed the simple things like having a cup of tea with family and friends, hugs and giggles from my little nieces and nephews. I was lonely so I took to the beach.

Along with Denver, my beach loving black lab, we walked the beach morning, noon and night. Denver never missing an opportunity to take a dip!!
We would often watch this small group of people swimming in the middle of winter, in all sorts of weather and they seemed to be loving it as much as Denver?

So, in early April 2021 I too took the plunge!! Being a summer swimmer, all my life (June, July and August) April was early for me but I did it and felt the power of the sea and how it made me feel, it is a feeling I will carry in my heart forever.

I finally plucked up the courage to ask to join the group of swimmers that had multiplied in size over time and things just got better for me. I have made many new friends, reacquainted with old and I can put my hand on my heart and tell you I have had swims that have touched my soul and healed my mind.

We are a unique bunch of people that help each other without even realising it, kind, caring and non-judgemental.

I have had powerful experiences with the right people at the right time. I have so much gratitude for all this swimming group has given me. An amazing group of people supporting each other through the power of the sea.

My wish is that future generations don't leave it to a global pandemic. Make it a part of your life and keep this wonderful group alive. We are blessed to have this on our doorstep, Youghal, the people of Youghal and its beautiful beach.

Siobhán O'Connell

This is the power of gathering:
it inspires us, delightfully,
to be more hopeful, more joyful,
more thoughtful: in a word,
more alive.

Siobhán O'Connell

RECIPES FROM OUR TABLE!

Christine Ryan

INGREDIENTS

3oz coconut
6oz self-raising flour
6 oz castor sugar
6oz unsalted butter
3 large eggs
½ teaspoon vanilla essence
4 tablespoons milk
Icing
Lemon juice
2 tablespoons icing sugar
3oz toasted coconut

METHOD

Grease and line a 9” square tin.
Cream butter and sugar until light and fluffy. Add rest of ingredients and blend well.
Pour into tin and cook well at 160 degrees.
Sieve icing sugar and slowly add lemon juice to make a pouring consistency.
Top cake with it and scatter with toasted coconut.

GLUTEN FREE CHOCOLATE BROWNIES

INGREDIENTS

3 large eggs
286g chocolate spread

1 x 8" square tin
greased and lined

Oven at 180 degree

METHOD

Beat eggs for at least 8 minutes until pale and doubled in volume. Microwave chocolate spread for 30 seconds. Fold chocolate by pouring slowly into egg mixture. Once fully combined, pour into tin and cook for 20 – 25 minutes. Check with a cocktail stick to see if it is cooked.

BANANA BREAD

INGREDIENTS

125g unsalted butter
1 cup castor sugar
2 eggs
3 soft overripe bananas
teaspoon of baking soda
half teaspoon of salt
1 and a half cups of flour

Grease and line a 2lb loaf tin
Oven at 180 degree

METHOD

Beat butter and sugar until pale and fluffy. Add eggs and mashed bananas. Then fold in flour, baking soda and salt. Mix well and pour into loaf tin.

Cook for 50-60 minutes. Cool in tin.

A FULL MOON

A full moon
In all its glory
Kisses the water
As it peeps slowly.

Above the horizon
The edge of never
Swimmers united
Moments captured forever.

What the moon teaches
There's beauty in darkness
A spotlight of hope
In the midst of mess.

The glow of orange
Magic in the sea
Surrounding us all
Time to just be.

Aisling Curran

NIGHT SWIM

BRAVING THE ELEMENTS

Braving the elements in the height of winter. The swims become dips in these extreme temperatures and it is a case of in and out. The swim involves scraping the ice from your windscreen to drive to the Front Strand.

Winter Swim

I swam in the depths
O the cold and the stones
My hands and my feet my ears and my bones
What brought me to this briny place
I feel the sting upon my face
Elation now I've overcome
The isolation and the numb
I feel alive I feel awake
I will return for my mind's sake

Biggs

I SWIM FOR ME.

For as long as I can remember, I swam every summer in the sea with my family. I would usually stop around the end of September. Last year I decided to continue sea swimming for as long as was bearable. It was becoming very popular.

I reconnected with some of my old friends and definitely made some great new friends along the way. We decided to keep swimming as long as we could and we did the full winter into spring and then summer. We found it exhilarating, refreshing and lots of fun. One of the best parts of the swim was having the cuppa and the chat after, it was a very important part of the swim as you could sit, say nothing and listen, or join in on the chat. You could just come for the swim and go or stay for a while. Everyone had their own reason for being there, nobody asked any questions.

I swim for me, it's exhilarating, the sensation you get when you hit the cold water, but then you get used to it and of course the screaming from everyone is brilliant. I swim in cold water because it feels good and I will keep doing it. We are all united in our sea swimming.

Life is for living,

P.

CONNECTIONS

All of us who live abroad (I have lived in the UK for 35 years) have a special connection to the sea. Swimming has always been a big part of childhood for most of us and I have very fond childhood memories of spending summers in Green Hole Beach and Claycastle, as well as the Slob Bank. As a regular visitor back home, through my sister, I have become an honorary member of the sea swimming community in Youghal. It has been a great way to meet old friends and make new some new ones as well. Although not a swimmer myself, it has given me a sense of connection on so many different levels – my childhood, the community, old and new friends – for which I am so grateful.

MOS

A PERFECT DAY FOR WILLIAM TREVOR

It was better to plan things. That way, you had something to look forward to, even if you slept badly in the night. Getting up early this September morning, the second such fine day in a row, was a relief. She felt exhausted, but after a quick visit to the shops, she decided to have an early swim. She greeted Seamus with the cheerful view that nobody but God could have made a day like this. There wasn't a single cloud in the heavens. Seamus agreed. "How many days, how many days without clouds could you count in your short lifetime, short though it has been, Susan, short though it has been?"

Seamus spoke in circles. He twined a small loin of pork on the counter and then let it dance on his palm as if to signal some potential that the meat contained. An arm extended. "God bless now, Mary."

"Thanks, Seamus — see ya now."

She was reading William Trevor on the beach later in the morning as the hot sun continued to raise rumours of an Indian summer. The tide was in. After her swim she was in that half-life between the electric thrill of cold and the rising satisfaction of heat. It was the moment when she felt most alive. The beach was quiet, the tide sat still like a painted lake. She had taken her usual spot in front of the row of Georgian houses, the furthest one of which belonged to her uncle. Kneeling, she spread her towel against the face of the concrete wall that marked a boundary between the vast Atlantic blue and the grey, untidy car park lurking on the other side.

She lay there, just above the beach, reading the novel. Her mind wandered and she paused to imagine the author in his younger days, how he had his home in the centre of Youghal and how he must have walked the sands in front of her. She wondered if he'd had a dog… but this thought led nowhere.

Thank God, Joe had made it back from the GAA fundraiser. It was a big affair and he would have had more than a few with John Jamieson and that gang. At intervals they would have shifted like cloud cover, in and out of the clubhouse to smoke outside. The banter would have grown louder as the hours ticked by, some of it ill-humoured, getting sharper with each return to the noise of the bar. She could hear the echoes of old, sharp conversations, like bits of shrapnel lodged in her memory.

She tried to block these voices out of her mind, but ever since she had gazed down on him this morning it had been difficult to erase the picture of her prone husband from her mind. How impervious he had looked.

Still, she felt great now, now that she was after her swim. Her body felt warmer and she had the awareness and serenity that comes after salt water. At first, it had felt a little bracing, but this was natural. East Cork was never going to be the Costa del Sol. She swam most days of the year, if she could and this was her choice spot when the tide ran in her favour. She hated the endless walk when the tide was out. Looking back from the sea, you felt you were miles out, even though you were only up to your knees! Like Alice, when she is impossibly tall. What an amazing thing the sea was, though, how daily it performed its magician's tricks and surprises.

The couple that disturbed her view had taken the early bus from Cork. Free travel was great. It gave elderly people the freedom of the country.
"Lovely morning."

"Isn't it beautiful though? We've only just got off the bus and we couldn't have picked a better day, I'd say."

The man was tall, a little overweight and Cork friendly. His wife was thin. He made an effort to please his wife and give her credit.

"Eileen got the weather right, didn't you Eileen? She was only after meeting a woman on the bus. Wasn't she in Spain for a week and didn't it rain all the time! And here we are and not a sinner on the beach. It's heaven, isn't it?"
"Isn't it though. You're dead right, it's heaven alright."

She heard them continue their conversation after this, as they put down their bags and spread out a large red tartan blanket, anchoring it with a flask of tea and a tupperware box filled with neatly cut sandwiches. Then something else in tin-foil.
"We'll be grand here, Eileen."

Once upon a time the beach would have sung on sun-drenched days like this one. There would be shouts, complaints and conversations in the lilt of Ballyvolane; whiter than white bodies; pink babies and wandering toddlers; young skinny fellas with hurleys and soccer balls; and others after drawing the lines of a tennis court on the flattened sand. Splashes from the ocean accompanied by shrill, sharp cries of nervous joy. On Sundays there were bigger crowds still. Fetched from the train in their hundreds, they appeared like refugees seeking the haven of the seaside. Radios blared along the promenade, Micheal O' Hehir voicing tense moments from Thurles where Cork were going all out against Tipp. The excitement would rise palpably when the commentator called the name of Seanie O' Leary. Another goal for the goal king. Another goal for Cork!

She heard a voice and looked up. The sun glared and she put her hand up to shade her eyes. She found it hard to see.

It was the man.
"I'm very sorry to bother you, Mrs., but I was wondering if you had been in for a swim, like?"
"I have, I have. It's lovely now. It's like a bath. She exaggerated a little.
He thanked her. His wife interrupted.
"Would you look at him? He hasn't been swimming in years and you wouldn't mind but he's been sick as a dog for weeks. He's had an awful cough and the doctor said he should be very careful."
"Still, the swim might do him good all the same?"
"Ah stop, Eileen. Amn't I fine, sure. And the water is lovely. I'll be in and down and out before you know it."
He was boyish and kind in his firmness.
"That fella," she joked, "he's never been down in his life!"
The wife laughed at her own joke. Feeling included, she laughed along.
Paddy Bresnan caught her eye as he marched smartly past with his two black labradors.
"Susan, lovely morning."
"Morning Paddy, 'tis long overdue."
"You're right. Make the most of it now."
"Indeed we will, Paddy."

Before going back to her reading, she noted that the man from Cork was in up to his knees. He was wearing red Adidas soccer shorts that looked far too young on him.

The novel, or was it a novella, was the book club's choice for this month. It was called Reading Turgenev. Joan reckoned it was one of the best books she'd ever read. She had dropped the book off with a recipe for gluten-free scones and said she couldn't stand the husband in it. Jesus, some men. Elmer, what kind of a name was that? Trevor's writing was like polished wood though.

Removed from the book by her train of thought, she latched its pages with her thumb and looked up.

The man was in up to his waist, past the point of no return. His shorts were no longer visible. He was peering down into the water, as if in the mood to spot a fish. Any moment now and he'd make the big decision. He might be doing what she did herself. She counted to ten and went for it. The shock of the water made her blow her cheeks repeatedly as she pushed her hands rapidly to fight the invasion of cold. On the full sea the sun sparkled and at the foreshore the shallows began to pronounce some lace-cream wavelets. Sure enough, there was a bare splash and he was down. He wasn't one to make a big fuss in his swimming stroke and he seemed content to let the seawater gently lap about him.

She was glad she didn't go out last night. She liked Joan, but the rest of them annoyed her. They got so stupid and giddy after a few drinks. And then their voices grew shrill with laughter. Lost in gossip, Carmel and that lot would have been talking about Peggy who had been diagnosed with something people could only mouth silently.

She caught herself staring out at the island. Paddy passed again, walking more briskly back towards town, his arms moving like semaphores.
The man was down and his face was in the water. His wife hadn't noticed; she was reading the Examiner.

"He's having a great time, he's like a teenager!" she called over to the woman. Her face was hidden behind the opened paper. She was glad that the man was enjoying his swim; he seemed nice.
The paper was lowered and the wife, a little sullen and removed, acknowledged the instruction to watch her husband.
"He is. I hope his cough doesn't get worse," she reprimanded and she snapped the paper over her face.
Didn't she want her husband to have some enjoyment?

God only knows what time he got in. A figure exploring the room, making breathy, grunting noises, had stirred her. Then, an ignition of snoring and the familiar smell of stale cigarettes and alcohol. She lay still, thinking to herself until the light changed outside the window. The birdsong hatched and called her to get up. She hoped the weather would be warm enough for a swim. She couldn't wait to escape into the kitchen and when the sun rose on the other side of the estuary, her mood brightened with it and she felt good as she made her second escape in the car. As she shifted into second gear, she felt her shoulders relax.

There were shouts suddenly. She turned to see, from the direction of the lifeguard station, two young fellas were sprinting and shouting. What was it? She glanced at the woman, who glanced back at her as they both rose to their feet.
The body in the water wasn't moving.

Jesus, Mary and Joseph, surely he was okay? She took some steps forward to get closer, but the shingled beach gave way and she had to put her arms out to steady herself. She didn't want to look, but she was staring. It was the only thing that she could do. She felt a sharp pain in her foot. The wife stood still. What was wrong? Wasn't he just doing the dead man's float? The two young lifeguards had turned him and now they were pulling and dragging the man onto the damp edge of the sand. Next one of them was pumping his chest and counting.

'Call an ambulance, quick!'

The urgency caught her unprepared. She wanted to say something or make a decision. She felt helpless, useless and scared. Was she responsible? Were they shouting at her? Why her? From where she was standing, she saw that his eyes were open, but there was no life in them, only a glassy stare that seemed to express mild surprise. Somebody called for an ambulance again and then everything went quiet. Nobody spoke to the woman. She was standing there alone, staring and unmoved, the Examiner still gripped awkwardly in her hand. What was she supposed to do?

Her feet felt the harsh, jagged beach stones as she limped across to speak to the woman. She allowed the pain to dress a wince on her face. It was sympathy and it was also pretence.

"I am so sorry. Is there anything I can do for you? My uncle lives up the way. You can sit down and have a glass of brandy. It's good for the shock."
"Thank you."
She hadn't heard.
She put her hand on a bent, bird-like shoulder.
"Is there anyone I can phone for you, anyone at all?"
"Well, why don't we sit down over here and wait for the ambulance?"
"Thanks."
"I'll just put my book down and I'll be with you."

As she walked back with the book, she felt the sun on her neck and the irritation of the stones' rough edges. She placed the book down on its back cover, but the pages flowered open. She caught herself disliking the woman. She wanted to stay and read; above all, she wanted to avoid her uncle, who was forever complaining that she never called to visit.

Brian Mulcahy

THE FRONT STRAND - A SPECIAL PLACE IN MY HEART

I have never known a time when I was not swimming in the sea. As a child our favourite spot was the place on the Front Strand in Youghal, where the sea swimmers now gather to swim all year round.

Towards the end of October 2020 I went to the Front Strand for a swim. It was windy, there was light rain and I thought this will probably be my last swim of the year. When I went down the steps to the beach, four or five swimmers were sitting on the ledge getting changed. Older than me,they all expressed an intent to continue swimming.

COVID lockdown was in place. I was introduced to the WhatsApp group. With the encouragement of others, I have continued swimming, almost on a daily basis throughout the year since then. What a revelation it has been. It is as if a completely new resource has been presented to me free of charge. The minute I hit the water, cares and concerns seem to flow away. I feel completely alive and immersed in nature. All is well with my little part in the world. Tasks which lie ahead of me for the day seem completely doable, solutions presenting themselves.

The sense of wellbeing, or as it is known among our sea swimmers, "the buzz," never fails to materialise. The camaraderie is wonderful. I have always felt great after a swim, but thought this joy was confined to the warmer months. How wonderful it has been to discover the benefits are available all year round.

The location at the Front Strand, where we swim, holds a special place in my heart. There were five of us children in the family, three boys and two girls, when I was growing up, six years between oldest and youngest. During the summer holidays, we were sent out of the house in the morning, with our towels and togs and instructions to meet our parents at lunchtime at this particular location on the Front Strand. They would then arrive out with a picnic, have a swim, feed us and return to work. If there was rain or wind, we had instructions to call to any number of houses on the Front Strand, where shelter and kindness and sometimes chocolate would be made available to us. It may take a village to raise a child, but the Front Strand in Youghal seemed to do it all by itself.

As I got a little bit older Monday morning was a time to meet the pals and collect the glass bottles left on the strand after the swarms of visitors on the previous Sunday. Each bottle was worth a penny as far as I recall when returned to Mr O'Neill's shop. I have a very distinct memory of sitting on the ledge under the seawall at the end of May 1975. Something clearly infectious had broken out in school and we were all sent home early. It was considered so important that the students facing their "Inter" and "Leaving" would be spared the contagion so our summer exams were cancelled. What a wonderful relief! Sitting on that ledge, allowing the warm concrete to dry me, the horrendous thought came to me – this time next year I will be starting my own Leaving. The only thing to quell the rising panic was another swim. The sea worked its magic again.

I consider myself blessed to have lived all my life by the sea. The smell of salt water, the sound of waves rolling, the sight of white horses jumping over the seawall, the call of a seagull, the clang of a lanyard against a mast mesmerise and excite me as when I was a child.

I am so grateful to my fellow sea swimmers for making this joy and excitement available on a daily basis all year round. Thank you one and all.

David Keane

ME, GRIEF AND THE SEA

I returned to life while struggling with the loss, writing/journaling (as I know it now) was my way to give time to the grief, the love that was lost. I wrote about my feelings, my thoughts, the challenges with both internal struggles and adapting to the world. The words encapsulated my daily life, while processing grief. I spent time getting to know my body, my heart, my mind, noticing how it reacts, letting the tears flow, noticing the numbness, owning the confusion, the battle in my mind and the ache in my heart. To take each moment, notice and accept my thoughts and feelings with compassion to allow me to go through the moment and not avoid it. By journaling I developed a language to describe my journey and come to terms with grief. It was a platform to be with my thoughts, my feelings and my body's sensations, understanding these allowed me to share my journey with my family and friends. When all is said and time has passed, the undercurrents of a love lost and grief still catches me. I am who I am when I meet the sea. The sea gives me perspective and strengthens my well grafted composure that shields my heart.

My name is Michelle, I had three pregnancies, we lost our daughter Zayna at 26 weeks pregnant in 2016, our son Malek at 32 weeks pregnant in 2017 and we had a miscarriage in 2021. I am grateful for my husband, family and friendships, they are my guardians who will weather any storm. The sea allows me to rebalance, to accept there is a greater force than me that to battle against nature is futile. The sea gives me strength to navigate life with grief and to live in honour of life.

Michelle

THE SEA

Thank you for what you give to me,
You are the constant,
A grounding perspective of simplicity,
You disarm all that society loads upon me,
A picture-perfect life that is not my reality,
You give frustration a voice,
An acknowledgement that this was not my choice,
You silence the screams and the roar,
A wave crashing gives space to explore.

You show strength in the complexity,
A force where I can surrender my fight,
You recognise determination in the calm,
A depth that warrants respect,
You are the reckoning of hopes and dreams,
A grounding of body, mind and soul,
You are a far-reaching vastness,
A calmness found in the horizon.

You are the sea and I am me,
A reset, A release, A moment of peace.
I own my love that grieves.

Michelle

THE PAINTER ON THE BEACH

For Patsy O'Mahony

You whisk the brush
Across the canvas

A winter wind
Billows above the sand

You whisk the brush
In a flash of light

Walkers look on
And gasp at your creation

You whisk the brush
In that familiar palette beat

Surfing waves of love
Our painter on the beach

Jordan McCarthy

THE CALL OF THE SEA

Deep in a slumber my mind is at ease, I freeze, the alarm breaks this restful reverie. Pulled back curtains reveal the day, cold, crisp, 'I'm on my way' I want to say. But fear takes its grip, the doubts, they seep they drip drip into my mind, 'You can't do this', the resolve unwinds.

Then ping, I reach for the phone, wise words displayed, I'm not alone. Warm towels that caress the extremities of my body impress upon the boots the gloves all shoved into the big grey bucket. Suck it up, I'm going in, the mantra in my mind begins and continues til I reach the shore. And breathe, don't freeze from the bite and the sight of the ice on the ground and the sound of my heart beating in my chest.

I do my best to undress right next to newly made friends of mine. All resigned to make that dash, commit to the splash of the wave for the brave are the only ones mad enough to behave like this! So in we go. At first slow. Watching our feet navigate the pebbles below. Up to my ankles the cold water strangles not just the flesh but the fear and the stress. Up to my waist I turn to face the bodies behind as they wade and they wind their way into the sea that's calling me to let go. Let go. Shoulders down, not a sound, only my breath... my breaths! They're fast and they're loud and the rest of the crowd seem too far away to come to my aid. A display of dismay in the water ahead dear God I should have stayed in bed! The dread quickly subsides as the pace declines and my breath slows down and now, I have found a rhythm. Breathe and stroke, breathe and stroke.

My head pokes out of the Irish sea as I cut through the expanse now enveloping me. My mind quietened, no longer frightened of the thoughts of the day, of the bills I must pay or words I must say, regrets I replay, they all drip drip away. A cliché? Some will say. The result of us all being locked away. But cliched I will be because the call of the sea has enchanted me.

Ruth Hayes

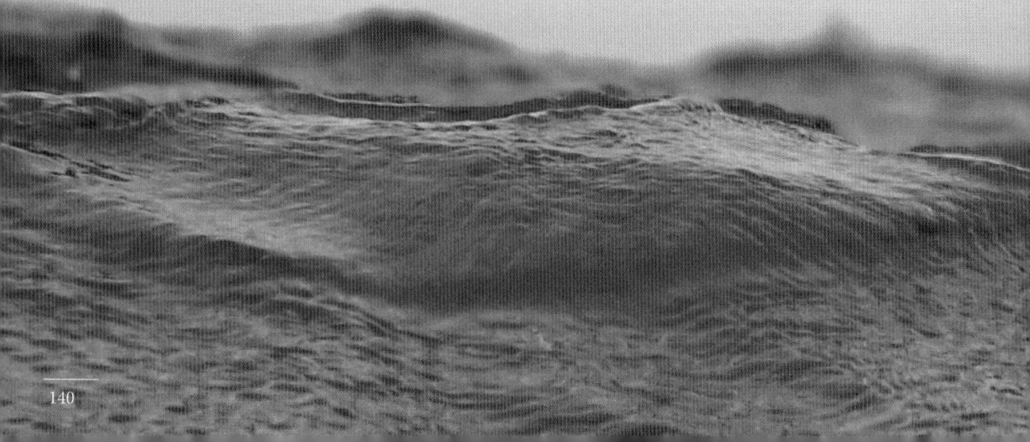

SWIMMING

Hunched shoulders
Muscles tight
Then you feel the cold wave
And all is right.

Into the salty white we go
Knowing how much
Peace will flow.

Laughter, shrieks
And lots of chat
The coldness fades
With all of that.

Leaving the sea
Calm and happy
Back tomorrow
For cold water therapy!

Aisling Curran

A SWIM THROUGH TIME

'Look at me, mam,' I yelled as I splashed and spluttered sea water from my lungs. My mother looked on, aghast, as she surrendered her only child to the water. As I wrapped my arms tightly around my uncle's neck, I clung on for dear life as we glided through the water. He was Neptune, the god of the sea and I was Nereid, a little sea mermaid eager to learn how to swim. This is my earliest memory of being in water. I was five years old and learning how to swim in Buttimer's Quay, Youghal. The quay was alive with youngsters who were like schools of fish that moved in sync with each other. I remember the fun, the excitement and fear as my uncles, Sean and Jim Hogan encouraged me to jump into the deep end of the quay, reassuring me that they were there to catch me. Each week I managed an extra stroke with every jump until I finally mastered the doggy paddle.

As I got older, I swam near Moby Dick's pub and braved the challenge of diving off the quay into an abyss of darkness. It was like diving into the underworld, into an invisible realm where hidden gems lay in the darkness of the sea. To a young person whose imagination was filled with adventure, magic and mystery, fuelled by fiction such as 'Twenty Thousand Leagues Under the Sea' and 'Treasure Island,' the quay became a treasure chest adorned with local artefacts. Over the years, I learned to move fluidly with the water, each stroke sliding past each other in a state of motion but all the time realising that I was connecting with something greater, a force of nature that entranced me. All I remember was that swimming felt good.

I swam in Green Hole and often looked up at the red brick of Loreto Convent which stood tall and poised, perched on the hill. However, there was an undercurrent in Green Hole, that unsettled me. It was the red flag flapping in the wind at the corner of the promenade that screamed danger to me. I have fond memories of building sandcastles there with my neighbours, the Calnans. Mrs. Calnan fed us buttered Marietta biscuits washed down with a cup of Tanora delicately balanced on shivering knees. Delicious!

As I approached the freedom of those teenage years, I ventured up the Lighthouse Hill and discovered swimming down the Divings. The waves had more energy here compared to the quays. I went from swimming in the Blackwater to the sea. There was something magical about swimming at the Divings, maybe it was looking up at the lighthouse standing steadfast, a beacon of light, a metaphor perhaps for all those who were feeling lost as they swam through time.

I finally ventured past Moll Goggin's corner and embraced the length and breadth of the Front Strand, which was also known as 'The Far Off' because it was so far away from the town. Miles and miles of silver sand and sea seemed to stretch forever but I finally found my spot to swim at The Gap. It was here that I savoured swimming with friends, sunbathing and diving off the old wooden breakers which have since almost disappeared.

The roars and screams from Perks filled the air. A spin on the bumpers was a novelty as it was half price every Thursday. The sweet smell of candy floss was my last purchase before I made my way home on my bike, pedalling as fast as I could down the Lighthouse Hill, my hair tossing in the wind as I left the sea behind.

I have wonderful memories of summers spent at the beach when Colin and I introduced our own girls, Sarah and Laura, to the joy of sea swimming. However, once September came, we put our swimsuits into hibernation until the following year. As the years passed by, my relationship with the sea changed and I preferred to walk on the strand rather than swim in the sea. There were many years that I did not swim but all this changed with the COVID-19 pandemic. The beach became our haven, a place to go to during those challenging times. I discovered an innate desire to swim in the sea again. Call it gravitation, call it freedom, the sea was like a magnet. On June 11th, 2020, I formed our sea swimmers' WhatsApp group to share swim times and sea conditions. This opened a window of wonder for me as I connected with my love of the sea again. Through the prism of social distance, we navigated our way forming a community of sea swimmers that we continue to nourish today.

My daily swims weave a vibrant fabric into the tapestry of my life. It is a time for me to reset my mind, to gain clarity and find balance. There are times when the water is freezing but I can now safely immerse myself in cold water and regulate my breathing which I find strengthens my resilience. The sea is our meeting point, sometimes a playground as we all bounce, splash and play with the waves. At times, the sea can be tumultuous not wanting us to swim or it can be a place of peace and calm that soothes and heals. Sea swimming has enhanced my wellbeing and encouraged me to savour the present moment and for this I am eternally grateful.

Linda Donoghue

WHY DO I GO SWIMMING?

As kids, we loved to swim and for the most part this was done in the pool, though not the pool that's there today! Our pool is the one out the Slob Bank. I grew up in Cork Hill and as a young boy, going out the strand was only done when your parents brought you, so we had to make do with the Slob Bank. We taught ourselves to swim and had great fun swimming from one side of the pool to the other, simple. We could walk out the bank, swim to the other side and go home via the boreen, through Murray Kitchens, into Jack Daly's field and home.

Many years later I got hooked on the sport 'Triathlon' which involved swimming, cycling and running, so now I had to learn to swim properly. What I enjoyed most about the sport was the longer distances in some of the events. I try to swim all year round, if I can, on weekends and two sessions during the summer.

We are truly blessed with the beautiful beach on our doorstep and the fantastic club that is South Coast Tri Club. We have the Ironman event in town which is fantastic. It is really great to see so many people cycling, running, kayaking, boarding, walking and of course swimming. Long may it continue!

Christy McCarthy

REFLECTIONS OF A NEWBIE

As a novice winter swimmer, I struggle to convert the various stages of the experience into words. First the apprehension: "It's too cold, I literally cannot even take off my clothes!". Then, determination: "I'm here now, I have to do it." Stripping off quickly and, if you're a serious planner, visit timed to coincide with full tide so there isn't too much of a build-up to total immersion!

Feet first, into the shallows… the COLD… but actually not as cold as I had feared. There are other people in the water (in wetsuits, not that I'm judging!) so I can't turn back now. It's windy, so the waves are big and breaking and I'm quickly splashed from head to toe. There's a moment of constriction as my body registers the cold; I breathe through this before I duck under up to my neck, jumping up again with a shriek.

The rubicon has been crossed; I'm here and I'm in.

I dive through the next wave and euphoria hits. I'm in my element. The water is cold but comfortable; the sun is shining and the sky is blue. Instagram informed me that the air temperature was 13°. It's blissful.

There's a kind of fizzing sensation coursing through my body as my internal thermometer works to regulate my body temperature in this new environment. I swim a few strokes of a front crawl then roll onto my back to just revel in the pleasure of being in the sea. It's not cold enough today to have to swim to keep warm; I can just enjoy it.

I dive through a few more waves and stay in longer than I did on my first dip last week, but I'm still new to this and I haven't yet learned how to judge my limits.

The wetsuiters exit and I feel I should too, particularly as the tide is fast reaching its height and getting close to the rock where I left my clothes!

Emerging from the waves (Ursula Andress, eat your heart out), I feel a powerful sense of achievement – a reminder that I can do whatever I put my mind to.

I don't feel cold. I collect my clothes from the rock and move to a step higher up, away from the marauding tide. I sit there in the sun in my wet togs for a few minutes.

It's wonderful. I need to do this more often. I want to swim in the rain, at sunrise, by moonlight and at every possible opportunity. I can never get enough of this feeling.

Tracey Kennedy

I FEEL BLESSED

I overheard my 4 year old out in the hall with her dolls one day saying "we are going for a dip." She then lay down and started kicking her legs and wriggling along the hall pretending to swim. Clearly in her mind it's a fun and normal thing to do with your friend, like my sister and I used to pretend with our dolls in the 1980s.

This is so exciting for me that sea swimming is a positive norm in society and I feel blessed to be able to be part of this community. I feel so grateful that we have the amenities in Youghal to swim regularly.

Growing up in Youghal I knew three ladies that swam everyday all year round, one was my Mother's cousin. It was ingrained in me that it was a healthy thing to do, of course they had no dry robes!

My summer childhood revolved around the Mall and the Front Strand. We were treading water and doing breaststroke from as young as six years. Every summer we did the Water Safety week. We swam in the Front Strand in the mornings and off the quays in the evenings with instructors for that week. From a young age we had a very rough tides calculation, we simply added an hour on from the day beforehand and if we were out the Front Strand as soon as the tide was almost in we could head for the Mall or the quays because it seemed like full tide was about one hour behind the Front Strand.
We loved it.

We spent hours in the sea just swimming and just like today, after the initial chill sensation once we "got down" we didn't feel the cold. I do remember that we used to find the sun very warm when we lay down on our towels to dry out but I guess it was because we were warming up from the cold, not that it was particularly warm. We also had a theory that the sea was warmer to swim in on rainy summer days, that the rain warmed the sea up. In addition to Water Safety week, you would have local fishermen mending their nets dockside.

We learned to respect the sea, much of which is written deeply in my subconscious: never swim alone, you could get a cramp or sting, never swim out and always swim parallel to the shore. We learned how to spot a landmark and to avoid areas with red flags flying like today. We watched the winds and state of the sea.

Twenty years passed and it's only in the last two years that destiny has brought me back to living in Youghal full time and fortunately I started dipping with a group. My main challenge is time. I don't have the time to go every day in winter but I treasure my Saturday mornings all the more. In the summer I do get to swim almost daily. Included in my fondest memories of sea swimming have been the winter and summer solstice swims of 2021 and 2022.

Mairead Boland

SUNRISES AND SUNSETS

The pandemic definitely opened up a door for me to something new that I never thought I would enter and that was swimming in the cold open water.

I'm a mum of four and a makeup artist and 90 percent of my work was wiped out by the COVID 19 pandemic. I had to keep myself positive throughout this tough time just like everyone else. I live in a small seaside town in the south of Ireland. A few summers before the pandemic struck I started to go for an early morning dip with my teenage daughter who loves swimming and sea jumping and she got me to join her. I started to like it. However, I can honestly say that while it was way too cold for me at the start, I truly enjoyed the feeling. I started sea swimming in the winter which was something that I would never have dared do, but I did get into it and very quickly became addicted.

I started to swim with a few friends in the sea near a beach in Cork called Redbarn and out of the blue, my husband said he would join me which was great and sometimes we would go for a swim during his lunch break from work. With my work I would often travel to West Cork and Kerry for weddings and we would bring our swim bucket with us and head to the beach near my working venue. That is the real beauty of living in Ireland.

I'm extremely grateful for the opportunity to see so many magical morning sunrises and evening sunsets and experience so many other great times in the sea. There is little to beat that great feeling of achievement every time we exit the water with big smiles and lots of laughs like giddy kids. Myself and my husband never thought something could have such a profound impact on our sense of life, sharing the time together and taking time from being parents and having a little break from our children each day and just enjoying US. Beaming with pride that we are among the few mad heads to get in the water in the cold winter months. For us it was such an important tool for making it through lockdown and for remembering that even during a pandemic, beauty is all around us.

It's up to us to enjoy and motivate ourselves to get up and push ourselves out of our comfort zone and to help us cope with the stressful aspects of our lives too. From there we got to know the Youghal Sea Swimmers' group and as they said "the more, the merrier". There is always someone swimming around the clock, so you're never alone in the sea from a safety point of view which is so important. Hi to all the fantastic Youghal swimmers and dippers. Meeting you and getting to know all of you and having such fun is something to remember forever.

I thank my lucky stars for the opportunity to meet the wonderful bunch of people at the sea.

Za McCarthy

I love the sense of freedom and feeling close to nature.
I enjoy floating on my back and gazing at the sky.
I feel lighter and invigorated after a swim in the sea.
Just makes me feel good.

Gaye

WE ARE SO PROUD OF OUR BLUE FLAG STATUS

The weather during the first spring of lockdown was fine and sunny. Some of us started swimming at the Front Strand in Youghal at the end of May. Apart from walking, it was one of the few things we were allowed to do. At that time we were mostly swimming around high tide. Then Linda suggested we start a WhatsApp group to keep in touch. This was the beginning of our wonderful group. The group has grown and grown since then and has been a source of fun and friendship for so many.

I have always swam in the sea but only during July and August and the odd time in September. The first year I gave up in October and didn't get back to it again until the 1st April, apart from the Christmas swim. Last year I kept it up throughout the winter.

I am amazed now, as we all are, that we've had this facility on our doorstep all these years, virtually unused. We are so lucky to have our miles of beach. This was especially appreciated during COVID times.

It is a great joy to get to the beach and have a few friends to swim with. Sometimes you might shiver as you get in but the experience is wonderful. And always you feel refreshed and invigorated. Sunshine of course improves everything! My morning swim gives a wonderful focus to my day.

I have always been very interested in environmental issues and completed the Coastwatch survey in the past. Last summer that survey was highlighted by the Youghal blue and green environmental group. A few of us swimmers decided to get involved. In the end Linda and I did the Coastwatch survey last October. This is carried out all around the coast and involves walking and carefully observing a 500m section. We did two of these sections, from Greenhole out as far as our swimming spot on the Front Strand.

We walked the beach at low tide, noting and counting any litter present. We examined the flora and fauna. We tested water coming in from some inflows for the presence of nitrates which would indicate the presence of sewage.

We found that this area of the beach was relatively clean, with plenty of living red, green and brown seaweeds on the rocky parts. We only found six pieces of litter including cans and a few bits of plastic. There were live mussels, limpets, barnacles, sea anemones and dogwhelks.

We were delighted to verify from our survey that our beach water is perfectly safe to swim in.

Sheila Sheehan

EXPERIENCES OF SWIMMING IN SEAWATER

My first encounter with seawater was back in the early seventies down on the slipway near where The Quay's Bar is nowadays. I started to learn to swim under the instruction of local swimming coach Sean Hogan, first learning to float and then grabbing hold of an old ESB pole that was on a chain support attached to the quay wall or the slipway.

The deep section of the dock was the next stage of developing your swimming skills. When at full tide, we had to slowly move into the deep section and back to the quay wall doing the breaststroke. When you realised that you were advanced to that stage, you were then taught how to float.

The following summer under the Irish Water Safety Association, I completed a course in swimming rescue, which over the next two years I won Intermediate and Senior Awards which was to prepare you to rescue anyone who was in a difficult situation and needed help.

In the mid to late 1970's I started swimming at Greenhole, straight across from the now Walter Raleigh Hotel. You experienced high tides and low tides. Depth of water was observed so you could swim safely within the boundary due to a red flag flying on a pole. Beyond this it was not safe to swim due to currents prevailing.

In the early 1980's it was out to the Front Strand promenade on which you continued your swimming and of course you were now dealing with big waves, plenty of seaweed, swimming here with crowds of people using the water, locals and visitors alike. A lot of experienced swimmers were evident here, good summers were rare, bar 1983, 1984 and 1989.

In the nineties, mixed summers were evident bar the heatwave of 1995, where literally thousands of people packed the beach. One day a few boys called out while I was swimming to retrieve their football which was floating out to sea. I tried to get it but soon realised when I looked back to the beach that I was gone beyond my depth. Luckily enough I spotted a local fishing boat just near a current, so I swam back to the beach only to hear the concern of the boy's father that I was gone out so far as the dangers of the sea were evident.

When in the water you learn about prevailing winds, which tides are going out and tides coming in. Of course in warm weather you could have jellyfish float nearby. What colour is on them, if golden brown probably not to fear them, but if the colour is blue or purple they are likely to sting.

You develop all types of swimming strokes, the breaststroke, the overhand and the backstroke. Floating on the water helps you to relax and conserve energy, which you need at times. I always found when coming out of the water to drink plenty of fluids, either bottled water or Lucozade to stop you dehydrating.

In the years 2000 onwards the seas were often rough. You experience powerful waves, always in September or early October - but you develop skills like diving through big waves before they land on you. You also learn to swim on the mountain of water building up and try to come in with the wave before it breaks up near the beach itself. There are places along the coastline around Ireland where surfers thrive on these conditions.

Now in the last decade and a half I have noticed the seawater getting warmer, ever before global warming arrived. It is like the current climate that we are experiencing now. At local level concerns about pollution around the harbour and coastline limited the liberty of swimmers to source a spot on the strand near Claycastle. The boardwalk is now nearby. As a result of people locally campaigning for a water and sewage treatment plant, finally a plant was up and running in 2017. A huge improvement in water cleanliness was evident so swimmers who were reluctant to swim in the area returned.

When COVID emerged with people outdoors more , a new wave of young swimmers emerged making the watersport so popular. A new event called the "Ironman" arrived locally with swimming included bringing along professional swimmers. Anyway as I conclude my experience with the sea I will always remain in amateur status.

Frank Tynan

SEA SWIMMERS

A night of laughter
And so much fun
A night to chat
And welcome everyone.

We sang and we danced
Our hands in the air
Making new memories
The night disappeared.

All drawn together
By a love of the sea
An ocean of kindness
Binding us easily.

Our Sea Swimmers group
A powerful force
Of friendship and love
Where hope overflows.

Aisling Curran

THIS FOR ME IS MY NEW NORMAL

I felt the only way to write this was straight after a swim/dip and what a day I picked. Being last minute dot com I had limited opportunities left and so rough seas it was! However these are some of the best ones, the crashing waves, the raw force of the sea and the power of mother nature. It's invigorating, exhilarating and I've never felt so alive. Obviously it has to be done safely, always with people and never when there's any risk to yourself. I always check and double check tides and test the force of the water before going in. I give myself five minutes just in my ankles, feeling which way the pull is and how strong the back wash or undercurrents are. This particular day I stayed in around my ankles and just lay down feeling the waves crash over me. I could feel the stress wash away and any anxiety lift as I moved completely into the moment. I love it. To say I'm addicted to it would be an understatement. I'm often found here at 6.30am, in the dark, in winter, in 0 degrees air temperature, but for me there is nothing like it for mental wellbeing. Something I can't get anywhere else. And it always works.

I've been sea swimming since I started triathlon in 2014 but it soon morphed into so much more. What was a sport turned out to be a leisure activity as well as a mental health tool. Going with groups of people, enjoying the chats, sharing your problems, letting go and having a cuppa of tea! I do both competitive swimming (lol if you can call it that!) and dipping and I find joy in both. I find with swimming (once I learnt to swim properly) I can go for ages, just in the zone, feeling myself relax and enjoying the calming effect on my mind. Dipping on wavy days is just a blast, the fun and the enjoyment with friends. I have to say the swimming community is just the best. You could be on any beach in Ireland and you'll always find a like minded soul to chat to (and I will definitely go seek them out lol). The social element, the mental wellness and the connection to nature really do help us humans navigate this crazy modern world. I'm a firm believer that we need to look back at our primal selves to help alleviate the modern anxiety and stress we have grown accustomed to and made normal. This for me is my new normal. This for me is living.

Tasha

DUCKING AND DIVING

I would not go so far as to say I am a sea swimmer , merely a sea dipper who loves to duck and dive between the waves!

There is a hardy network of like minded sea swimmers that once the summer sun has faded away will see no reason to stop and often the colder the sea becomes, the more powerful the effects it has both on your mental and physical state. The adrenaline rush that comes once you're submerged in cold water can stay with you for many hours after, that release of endorphins and serotonin can set up your day to be a beautiful one.

The sea salutes you when you are at your best and embraces you with a hug when you are at your worst and never judges, just accepts you in the here and now.

Come-unity. Coming together and uniting by the sea, breathing, moving, chanting, screaming, laughing and swimming in a circle invites a special kind of energy, especially on those cold mornings, when you really need each other for moral support.

So here's to all the wild salty souls who brave the waves each and every day.

May we always lift each other up and jump into the sea together. The sea makes you resilient and you can achieve anything.

I climbed Croagh Patrick with Helen and Nuala in May 2023.

Karen Hannon

BREATHE ME IN

Sea swimming during a pandemic offered a unique experience during the 5km travel restrictions. The ocean provided a calming atmosphere and a sense of peace during a difficult time in my life. I absolutely hate the cold so jumping into the freezing cold Irish sea was certainly not an appealing thought for me. When my friend Maria invited me to join her for a swim, I quickly realised the benefits that sea swimming has to offer. Swimming in the sea can be invigorating, therapeutic and calming all at once. It can also help to reduce stress, improve mood and even increase self-confidence. After a few basic lessons with Imelda Lynch who has swum the English Channel, I began to swim longer distances with some of the organised groups. I could see how swimming in groups provides a sense of community and support to people.

I was inspired by this new world that I had discovered at my local beach at Oysterhaven. I could see how enriching this was for my community so much so that I was inspired to create my first short documentary. I wanted to shine a light on a special person in the community who was helping hundreds of people in my area. My short film Muirdhreach features an interview with Imelda Lynch and the local sea swimmers of Oysterhaven. When the screening happened at the Tracton Arts Community Centre many of those who were featured swimming in the film were invited and enjoyed seeing themselves on the big screen

I am currently studying the Irish language hence the Irish title of my film Muirdhreach, which means Seascape in English. When it came to choosing the music for this short documentary I was delighted when one of my own original songs that I wrote and recorded a few years ago worked so perfectly with the film. The film opens with Irish spoken poetry taken from my song lyrics. I have enjoyed the entire process of earning how to produce, direct and edit a short film about sea swimming.

I had no idea when I started sea swimming last summer how much it could impact my lift. Connecting with nature and enjoying the ocean's beauty is something which has taken me a lifetime to discover. It's never too late to start. Sea swimming brings a sense of freedom and an escape from everyday life. For me it makes me feel connected to the world in a way that nothing else does. When we keep our minds open to new possibilities it can bring much fun, inspiration and positivity into your life.

Lorraine Hogan

Breathe Me In

A masterpiece of pleasure and pain
a beauty they can't contain
pulsating rhythm take a deep breath
inhale the scent of life and death

Aoibhneas lán le só is pian
Áilleacht í atá gan srian
Rithim chuisleach, glac d'anáil
Bolaigh cumhracht beatha 's báis.

Breathe me in, I'll breathe you in
Breathe me in. Complete my skin

Análaigh mé análód tú,
Análaigh mé d'fhonn mé a shlánú

Save me from solitude
no fear just let me fall
weightlessly I gravitate
bound to you lose it all

Tabhair slán ón uaigneas mé
Gan eagla, scaoil lem lámh
Imtharraingt éadrom dom stiúradh
Nasctha leat cailliúint iomlán

Lorraine Hogan

What Swimming Means to Me

My name is Mary Noonan from Grattan Street, Youghal. I am 76 years old. I have been swimming since I could walk. My mother always swam from April to October. She had some friends who swam with her, one in particular was Alice Daly who swam all year round at 6.30am down in Paxes Strand and then went over to 7am mass in the convent. The men used to swim at the diving rocks, no women would dare go down there. I remember Joe Hallissy from Ashe Street and Michael Joyce from Windmill Hill. The men would never bring bags just equipped with a towel and bathing suit. Everyone would know they were going swimming with their towels under their arms.

Swimming was a natural thing to do in our house, like getting dressed or going for a walk. It was natural. I still find it very therapeutic and relaxing. If you are stressed, or worried about anything, go for a swim and all is well. Just sit for a while and observe nature, listen to the sound of the waves and all is well. When we were swimming years ago there was no protective clothing, just a bathing suit and a towel. People would play pranks on each other. When you were swimming your clothes would be gone when you came out of the water. One would have to walk home only with a towel and swimsuit as there were very few cars around then. It was all in jest. Clothes could be left back the next day when you went for your swim. I have no photos of that time because no one would stand in bathing suits for a picture. Very few people had cameras as back then they were a novelty.

Mary Noonan

MY MOTHER PACKED SANDWICHES...

As a child our parents took us swimming every evening. My mother packed sandwiches, there were seven of us and we all went swimming. As my older siblings moved away it was just my younger brother and I. I was always the last one to come out of the water. My mother's voice shouting, "We're going, come on, we're going." They couldn't get me out of the water!

Later I got married and brought my own children swimming to the strand. Then, when I was working, my dad brought my children to the same place that I went with my parents. I joined him several times and we would reminisce. I gave up swimming after that for years until the pandemic came and I started swimming again on my own until I met one of the sea swimmers and she said to come along. To my amazement it was the same place that I went as a child with my parents and where I went with my children. Now, I'm back swimming again in the same area. I find great friendship and companionship in the sea. What a beautiful place to be!

Kay

THE SOUND OF THE SEA

If you ask people what they think is the sound of the sea, they will probably mention the buzz of spilling waves, the bang of dumping barrels, or else the gusts of the onshore breeze. However, if you ask someone who regularly puts their face down in the water to swim or even just dip, they will tell you anything from a song that had been stuck in their head since yesterday, to a quiet self-talk about their recent difficult conversation with a friend, to absolutely nothing at all…

My name is Filip. As I write this testimony, I am 26 years old. I was born in Poland and moved to Ireland with my mom and younger sister, Gosia nine years ago. Of all the places in Ireland, we chose to move to the small town of Youghal, where my eldest sister, Agata, lived with her husband and daughter. Before we emigrated, Gosia and I used to spend our summer holidays in Youghal. Every long continental winter I longed to be back in Ireland for my sea adventures alongside Agata who worked here with her husband as beach lifeguards. Poetically enough, Gosia and I ended up working on the same beach for five and seven summer seasons, respectively.

Even after we moved to West Cork, every summer we both came back to Youghal for beach lifeguarding. There was simply something tantalising about this place. Through years of hardships at school where we could not understand what people were talking to us, through the stresses of college exams, through a multitude of follies and wrong decisions that young adults simply have to commit, the sea was our escape. Language was not a barrier, college seemed to have perished, whatever stupid things we did (always after 2am) were shared with the best friends who had the same passion for the sea and lifesaving.

As a scientist with a Bachelor's and Master's degrees in Human Physiology, I can name a vast number of health-related benefits that come from swimming in cold sea water. Immersing full body in cold water reduces inflammation, boosts our immunity, restores balance of our nervous system, maintains our motivation by increasing the release of dopamine in our brain, improves our metabolic health and even converts our excess white-type of fat, into the metabolically active brown fat. Did you ever wonder why children can stay in the sea for hours? Primarily because we are born with large deposits of brown fat that burns energy to generate heat. In that way, our vulnerable cubs can literally heat themselves up in case they had no fresh set of rompers or a fleece blanket. Like little furnaces. This is why I love the sciences of physiology and evolution; every small feature of our body allows us to adapt to our surroundings and survive.

However, my love for the sea cannot be summarised by the science of cold-water immersion or cardiovascular conditioning that comes from open water swimming, sailing, surfing and so on. I love technology. It allows us to propel medical science, treat previously untreatable diseases and improve athletic performance. Everything I deeply care about as a scientist and an athlete. Sadly though, the rapid progress of information technology is potentially disfiguring our natural sense of community and belonging as a human species. We are more connected yet disconnected at the same time than ever. We want more, but we don't really know what. We seek approval of a phantom adjudicator.

Early this year I believed that the judgeful eyes of every single person are one me. If I don't meet the expectations from myself as a scientist and a triathlete, I will be mocked and cast away from my communities, groups of friends and family. However,a couple of weeks ago, after a long break from surfing, I decided to surf at the Front Strand beach. I was out in the stormy sea on my own. I got knocked over by a 6-foot wave. After I resurfaced from the whirlpool and got back out to safety, beyond where the waves break, a thought came to my mind. I realised that I could do it all day. Balancing between life and death and simply taking pleasure in the fact that I am only a little piece of cells in this vast reservoir of life, the sea. I realised that the sea does not care whether I receive a doctoral stipend or win an Ironman race. I am just a small part of this transparent matter that gave rise to all life on Earth. And I am ever so happy to be here, alive.

Thank you for letting me hear your voice.

Filip Kolodziej

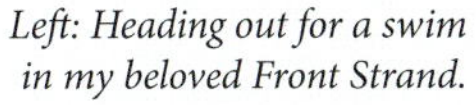

Left: Heading out for a swim in my beloved Front Strand.

Right: My dad, our idol sister, Agata, me, and my "baby" sister, Gosia ahead of the Christmas Swim in our new home, in West Cork.

TRIATHLON - WATER BABY

From a young age I have always been a water baby. From initially learning how to swim in the swimming pool and then in the Blackwater River in Fermoy. It was after this at about 12 years of age that I found sea swimming. I started to go down to my aunts in Youghal initially during a summer and absolutely loved the sea, the waves, the sand and the smells that really helped you feel at one with nature and from that point on with the last 30 years I head to the sea as much as possible. I find sea swimming very therapeutic and only recently realised just how much it helps to regulate your breathing. This is something I practise now when in the water to help regulate it for my fitness and health. I have completed many sea swimming distance events and also many triathlons where the sea swim was the first event. As I've retired from triathlon now I just go down for a swim and mostly just to feel the cold water waves and the connection to nature, it really is one of my happy places.

Anthony Kenny

FAMILIARITY

Like many of the Youghal Sea Swimmers, I have had the pleasure of dipping in the sea for quite some time. In fact, I can safely say that contact with the sea water began so early in my childhood that it constitutes an integral part of my earliest memories. On reflection, I have come to realise that I was blessed with parents and siblings who valued the great resource that our shared coastline is and the tremendous benefits, both physical and psychological, to be derived from frequent contact with the sea. Thus, as a child, I became familiar with the numerous beautiful beaches and coves, both east and west of my native city, which we are endowed with here in Co. Cork. Not that my familiarity with our coastline could be described as parochial. On the contrary, my late mother being a native of Waterford, ensured that I became equally familiar with the stunning Déise coastal features from Ardmore to Dunmore East and on to Wexford's Duncannon.

I would like to think that I have imparted some of this love of sea and coast to my own offspring. My beloved late wife and I were blessed with three children and from an early age, strove to give them an appreciation of the benefits of sea swimming combined with an awareness of the ever present danger which tidal waters pose. As a young family we were frequent visitors to Youghal and for a number of years, availed of a local mobile home during the summer months. This facility afforded us the opportunity to go sea swimming on most days and thus began, for me at any rate, a practice which has culminated in daily exposure to the brine throughout the year. In this regard, I must acknowledge the initial and ongoing support and encouragement of the Youghal Sea Swimmers, without whom, I should never have braved the icy winter waters in the first instance. Needless to say, there have been frosty mornings in the depths of winter when I wished I were anywhere other than the Front Strand wondering why I ever fell in with this crazy troupe!

Since my family and I took up residence in Youghal on a permanent basis some years ago, the daily camaraderie and good cheer of our fellow swimmers have been much appreciated and never more so than during Carmel's long and difficult illness and on the occasion of our great loss. Personally, I can say that the challenge of facing the first steps and whatever the sea hurls towards us every morning, though never easy, has had a deep significance. Taking that daily challenge as part of a group of like minded souls has, for me, made all the difference. There has never been a day when, physically or spiritually, I have swum alone. Deo Gratias!

Long may the community of Youghal Sea Swimmers survive and thrive.
Ní neart go cur le chéile.

Barry

LEARNING TO LOVE THE SEA

My mother took us as children and our friends too, on the short walk from our house down to Sandycove Harbour in Dublin every day of the summer holidays. She would sit with a flask of coffee on the sand, under the shadow of the James Joyce Tower and we, as toddlers and small children would paddle in the sea. Then we progressed to swimming lessons, at Sandycove Baths, with the extraordinarily progressive Miss Gillmore, whose enthusiastic mentoring of children in swimming was ahead of her time. "Up, out, together" she would intone as she instructed us to master the breast stroke. My mother would still be there, with the towels, flask of coffee and watchful eye, as we then progressed to Dun Laoghaire Baths, where Miss Gilmore actually got some of us to dive off the "high board".

My mother told me one of her few regrets in life was that she never learnt to swim, much as she loved the sea and lived most of her life beside it. So, she was determined that her children would learn to have the courage and enthusiasm to dive in and enjoy it. Her legacy has passed on not only to her children and their friends, but also her grandchildren. Now as sea swimming has become so popular all over the Irish coast, I often wonder if any other children who grew up in south county Dublin like me decades ago remember Miss Gilmore?

Loving the sea was always in the family. My great uncle on my father's side swam every day of the year in Dalkey, while he was most of his life involved in Ireland's fight for independence. He wrote about it in his autobiography, A Leaf in the Wind" and said swimming gave him strength and courage throughout his long and healthy life.

In Ireland we have some of the best beaches in Europe and I have enjoyed many of them - from Donegal to Sligo, Kerry and Cork. And for the past number of years enjoying the beautiful beach in Youghal, I have to say for me now it is the best. We are so fortunate to have it on our doorstep and every year more and more people are enjoying swimming in the sea here. It soothes the soul, mends the broken hearts, leaves us smiling again and makes us all better.

Mairéad Robinson

WALKING WITH ELVIS

I have special memories of my beloved father and his love of water. During the summer, packed with biscuits and Tanora, my father would drive Sarah, Laura and myself to the Front Strand. He would continue towards Claycastle to join his friends from Cork. They were his former colleagues from Fords and Dunlops. The city boys would travel by bus to Youghal to swim in the sea with him. My father Dinny was a pure Corkonian from the Lower Road and always availed of the opportunity to catch up on the gossip from the city.

My father loved to walk along the quays in Youghal and out the Slob Bank with Elvis, his faithful companion. The scene was captured in this tender photograph and was gifted to my father by Neasa, a family friend. When my father was in hospice care, he displayed this image at the end of his bed and loved to recall walking with Elvis along the quays on a magical misty morning.

Linda Donoghue

WHAT SEA SWIMMING HAS DONE FOR ME

I swim with a group in Garryvoe known as the Sea Swimmers. I am a 58 year old with rheumatoid arthritis and I have been swimming in the sea every day for nearly 2 years. The benefits I get from it are:

It reduces inflammation in my body.

Regular swims improve mood, energy and ease stress.

This activity helps to provide good health and happiness.

It is a great social activity and you get to know many people.

It doesn't cost a lot.

Anonymous

KAY – AN ORIGINAL SEA SWIMMER

TO DIP OR NOT TO DIP!

For me in my youth swimming was something we did on a hot day in the summer – little did I know that swimming now is part of my daily routine just as important as breakfast! Every day the conditions are different from a sea of white horses to a sea of glass. One thing that hasn't changed is the friends I have made since beginning my daily swim routine for which I am forever grateful. Long may it continue.

Ita

Alfredo

Oscar & Buttons

Roxy

Sandy
Shelby
Archie

SWIMMERS GO INTERNATIONAL: VIVA LA FRANCE!

In June 2023, twenty four of Youghal's community of sea swimmers were invited to travel with a delegation from the Youghal Twinning Association to Larmor Plage, a town in Morbihan in Brittany, France as part of the twinning exchange.

The Youghal swimmers were delighted to accept and made connections with a French swimming group called L'etoile de la Mer (Star of the Sea). This connection was nourished throughout the five day visit. The Youghal swimmers enjoyed memorable swims with the Larmoriens. They swam in several beaches in Larmor Plage, Kerguelen and Toulhars. This of course was followed by the traditional petit dejeuner of fresh croissants from the local boulangerie as the aroma of the café wafted through the warm sea breeze. and coffee on the beach.

The French Twinning Association coordinated many activities for our group throughout their visit. The highlights included a visit to the Oceanopolis Aquarium in Brest and a tour of the Sailing Valley in nearby Lorient. They also visited the old walled port town of Vannes as well as having the opportunity to walk the sandy beaches of Larmor Plage. International friendships were formed between the Irish and French through their mutual love of the sea. The swimmers had a wonderful trip and look forward to welcoming the French swimmers with the French Twinning Committee (Le Jumelage) to Youghal in 2024.

OPEN WATER SWIMMING TIPS

1 **BE PREPARED.**
Check the weather and tides, choose your spot, go with a buddy, have the right equipment.

2 **IF IN DOUBT, DON'T GO OUT.**
No matter how much preparation you do, or how experienced you are, if a swim doesn't feel right there is no shame in getting out of the water straight away, or not entering.

3 Make sure you **ACCLIMATISE** to avoid cold water shock.

4 **BE SEEN.**
Wear a bright coloured swim hat and take a tow float.

5 **STAY WITHIN YOUR DEPTHS.**

6 **FLOAT TO LIVE.**

7 **CALL 999 OR 112**
and ask for the Coast Guard in an emergency.

NEVER SWIM ALONE

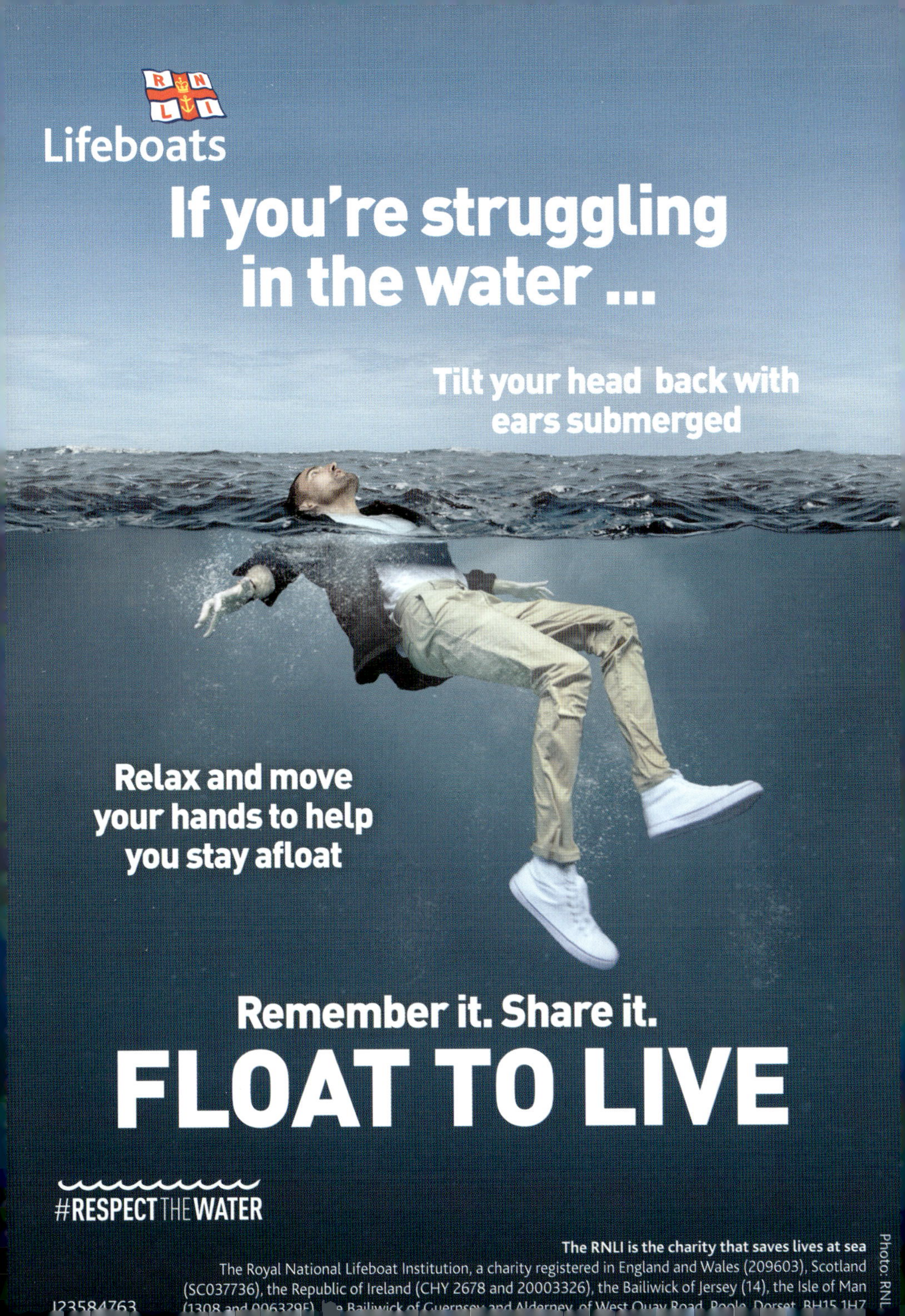

Lifeboats
If you're struggling in the water ...
Tilt your head back with ears submerged
Relax and move your hands to help you stay afloat
Remember it. Share it.
FLOAT TO LIVE
#RESPECTTHEWATER
The RNLI is the charity that saves lives at sea
The Royal National Lifeboat Institution, a charity registered in England and Wales (209603), Scotland (SC037736), the Republic of Ireland (CHY 2678 and 20003326), the Bailiwick of Jersey (14), the Isle of Man
Photo: RNLI

MIDSUMMER ARRIVAL 2023

SEA LOVER

At first your touch is shocking
Chilling my body as I immerse myself
In you.
My temperature drops to match yours;
A mutual connection.
You creep up my body
I slip down into you
You lift me gently and carry me
Where you please.
Sometimes I struggle
And try to impose my will on you
We both know how that ends.
Today I surrender
Relax and accept your caress
Weightless and peaceful in your hold
Eyes closed as the voyeuristic sun
Watches overhead,
His warmth is a contrast to your chill.
My heart rate drops,
The world fades,
You fill my body and soul.
There is only you,
And me in you,
I am yours.

Tracey Kennedy

AND BREATHE

Her Healing

She calls me when I'm low.
Roaring out, she's a force
I can't reckon with
And every time she beckons;
I go.

She holds me close,
Keeps me afloat.
So devoted
She's been doing this
For years.

Washing my tears,
Quashing my fears.
Every wave of emotion
Drifts until
She lifts it.

Throws it all away
Against a shore of rolling stones.
Then reassures me with
Another surge that
Feels like love.

And every time she calls my name,
She's trying to set me free.
And all I do is answer to
The healing of
The sea.

Eoin Coyne

Swimmers by
Andrea Cashell

Stones by
Andrea Cashell

Waves by
Andrea Cashell

Northern Light, Sea Road Paintings
by
Patricia Burns

Courtesy of Taylor Galleries, Dublin

ACKNOWLEDGEMENTS

Compiling this book was harder than we thought but more rewarding than we could have ever imagined. Our community of sea swimmers has formed such a wonderful connection with both the sea and each other that it is only fitting we capture this in a collection of personal stories about the sea.

Like the sea this book evolved over time and it is important to acknowledge those who helped in this evolution.

Thank you to Cork County Council Community Fund and Youghal Credit Union for their generous support. Thank you to Flanagan Print for their co-operation in bringing this book to fruition.

A special thank you to Eva- graphic designer for her professionalism, patience and amazing creativity.

Thank you to Andrea Cashell for allowing us to showcase her beautiful artwork on our front and back cover.

A huge thank you to all those who shared and submitted their own personal stories, poetry, photographs and artwork. Your contributions are much appreciated.

Thanks to Our Book LegaSEA Committee.

The creation of this book has been a labour of love. A journey of connections which took endless hours, copious cups of tea and lots of laughter.

Thank you to our families for your unwavering support, your patience and your love.

Jo Breslin, Catherine Davis, Linda Donoghue, Martina Hooley & Ita Treacy

CONTENTS

AUTHORS

PHOTO & ARTWORK CREDITS

Eílis Coogan 2
Catherine Davis 4
Michelle Ryan 6
Will McGoldrick @willshootfirst 7
Martina Hooley 9
Martina Hooley .10
Jo Breslin 11
Martina Hooley 12-13
Martina Hooley .17
Martina Hooley .18
Treacy Kennedy .20
Clockwise; Maurice Cronin Photography, Martina Hooley, Maurice Cronin Photography, Martina Hooley 22-23
Top to bottom;
Martina Hooley , Liam Davis 24-25
Catherine Davis .26
Catherine Davis .29
Michael Hussey. .31
Linda Donoghue. 33
Courtesy of Horgan Photos. 34
Liam Cooper 35
Catherine Davis .37
Katherine Keyte 38-39
Catherine Davis .41
Lino Print by Bobby Klang 42
Submitted by Carol Murphy 43
Submitted by Martina O'Halloran 44
Searlait Doyle 45
Catherine Davis .46
Kelly Motherway 47
Ewan McCarthy @dronesnapyoughal 48-49
Catherine Davis .50
Submitted by family 53
Submitted by family 54-55
Submitted by family 57
Photos courtesy of Horgan Photos. . 58-66
Submitted by Bernadette Barber 67
Catherine Davis .68
Tina O'Driscoll 70
Artwork by Paula Dunne 71
Martina Hooley .72
Martina Hooley .74
Submitted by Billy C. 75
Maurice Cronin Photography and Youghal Sea Swimmers 76-87
Sally O'Connor 88
Andy O'Donnell .89
Maurice Cronin Photography and Youghal Sea Swimmers 90-91
Catherine Davis .93
Catherine Davis .95
Catherine Davis 96-97

DISCLAIMER

Open water swimming by its nature presents risks to the swimmer over and above those found in a swimming pool.

Please note, we will not be held legally or financially responsible for any accident, injury, loss or inconvenience as a result of the informative elements contained in this book.

These articles are purely based on people's own memories. Many of the swim spots mentioned in this book are no longer considered safe to swim at.

We advise adherence to WATER SAFETY IRELAND guidelines in relation to all swimming activities and swimming spots. See watersafety.ie for more information.